Lorraine Farrelly

The Fundamentals of Architecture

Contents

How to get the most out of this book

The Fundamentals of Architecture is intended to be a solid foundation for those who work, develop and study within architecture. Through guidance, photography and illustration, key areas of architectural concepts, contexts and developments are covered. This book offers a unique resource and insight into the practical, philosophical and professional world of architecture.

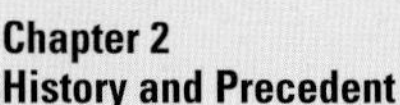

34

The Fundamentals of Architecture | History and Precedent

Design and innovation builds on precedent, on ideas and concepts that have evolved over time. Architecture uses precedents from social and cultural history and applies these influences to contemporary buildings, forms and structures. Having a historical understanding of buildings is an essential part of architectural design because it allows a relationship between the material, physical and formal developments that have been previously explored by other architects. Reacting against, or responding to these ideas has been the basis of architectural evolution.

35

Understanding Landscape < **History and Precedent** > A Timeline of Architectural Influences

1

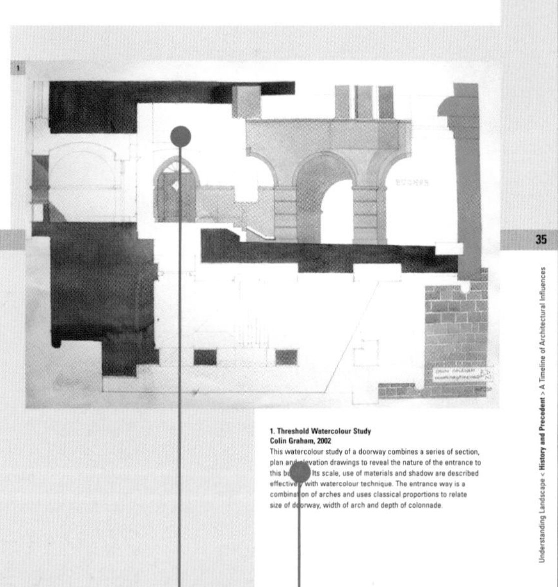

1. Threshold Watercolour Study
Colin Graham, 2002
This watercolour study of a doorway combines a series of section, plan and elevation drawings to reveal the nature of the entrance to this building. Its scale, use of materials and shadow are described effectively with watercolour technique. The entrance way is a combination of arches and uses classical proportions to relate size of doorway, width of arch and depth of colonnade.

Chapter introductions
Provide a brief outline of the key concepts and ideas that the chapter will explore.

Images
Photographs, diagrams and illustrations from an array of professional practices bring the text to life.

Captions
Supply contextual information about the images and help connect the visuals with those key concepts discussed in the body copy.

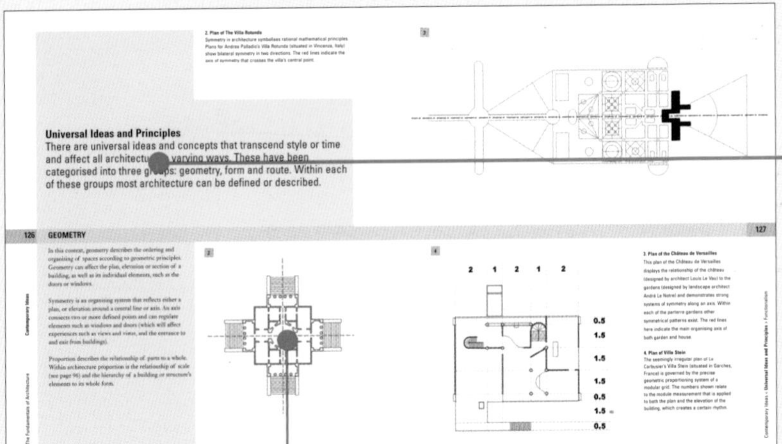

Section introductions
Each chapter section represents a different unit or area of study. The section introductions signify the start of a new unit and briefly outline what will be discussed.

Diagrams
Help to explain architectural theory and concepts in more detail.

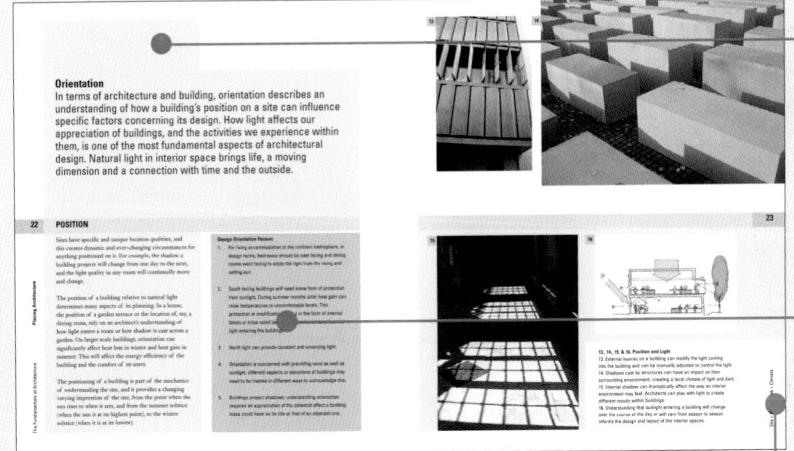

Colour coding
Denotes the chapter.

Box outs
Contain more detailed and contextual information about those architects or practices that are referred to in the body copy.

Navigation
Chapter navigation helps you determine which chapter unit you are in and what the preceding and following sections are.

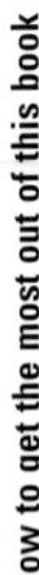

Introduction

Architecture

1. The art or practice of designing and constructing buildings.
2. The style in which a building is designed and constructed.

Describing architecture as 'fundamental' might suggest that there is a simplicity that underlies its expression. Architecture is a language that we understand because we inhabit buildings, they surround us and create our world. To achieve a piece of architecture requires engaging with a process of thinking, drawing and designing, a process that ultimately produces a building.

This process begins with an idea or 'concept' that relates to a particular site or context. It further develops (through a 'brief') into a 'form', which will have functions or activities associated with it. This form is then further developed structurally (as a frame or system), and materially (with a 'skin' or 'wrapping'). It is finally realised, framing experiences of light, sound, space.

The etymology of the word 'architecture' can be defined as *arkhi* meaning chief and *tekton* meaning builder or carpenter. This definition demonstrates the fundamental basis of architecture. As chief builder an architect needs to have an overview of building, both as an object produced and as an activity of construction. This overview requires an understanding of the context of buildings (which can be a landscape or the city, or somewhere in between), and an understanding of the building itself, in terms of its underlying concept or idea, its functions or uses and its materiality and structure. This overview, however, exists at many levels and the next stage of understanding of building is as a series of rooms, connected spaces that lead from the outside in. Further consideration is the control of light and sound in those rooms and the furniture that inhabits the spaces. The architect is a designer whose remit ranges from the large scale of designing a city to the smaller scale of designing a chair.

Architecture, as many other design disciplines, starts with concepts or ideas that initiate the creative process of thinking. These concepts can come from other (past or present) forms of architecture or architects, or from metaphors or analogies. These analogies can be to form: the structure of the Scottish Exhibition and Conference Centre in Glasgow for example, has a shape and skin which resembles that of an armadillo.

1. SECC Conference Centre, Glasgow, Scotland
Foster + Partners, 1995–1997
This building has a strong profile on its site along the River Clyde in Glasgow. The centre has a curved aluminium roof, which looks much like the hard shell of an armadillo, suggesting a strong, formal metaphor for the building's form and shape.

At its simplest form, architecture can be about designing spaces or rooms, or, at its most complex, designing buildings, streets and cities. The techniques involved in thinking about designing a chair or a room, at one end of the scale, or a city at the other, are varied and complex. Sometimes, they can be two dimensional and measured, for example, using drawings to a particular scale. At other times, the technique employed needs to be freehand and intuitive, allowing a more 'blue sky' kind of thinking. Whatever technique is deemed best for a particular stage of a specific project, all are essential to allow the incremental development of the design idea of the architecture.

1

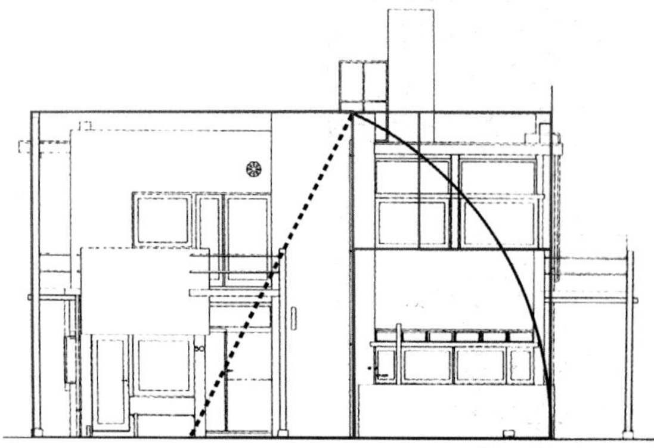

Architecture is about form and space making, but it also deals with function and how function affects form. This separates the principles of architecture from those of sculpture. As well as the form dealing with activities or functions, it also has to contain light, sound, heat and respond to a range of other issues that make an environment comfortable for human habitation.

Architecture sits in a place or context, in a 'site', which will affect its design and development in terms of orientation, views to and from the building and how it relates to other structures around it. Architecture can also be symbolic and have meaning associated with it; this could be religious, a cathedral for example, or an association with national identity, such as government offices. All significant cities have architectural icons associated with them, from the Eiffel Tower in Paris or the Petronas Towers in Kuala Lumpur, to the Chrysler Building in New York and the Houses of Parliament in London. Architecture helps people to identify with places and cultures, and buildings can have an impact beyond the user's physical experience of them.

2. Sketch of the Schröder House
This student drawing shows a geometric analysis of the Schröder House. When laid over an elevation drawing of the building, it shows how each element is proportionally connected. The red lines show the incorporation of the Golden Section (see page 117), which is a geometric proportioning system.

3. The Schröder House, Utrecht, The Netherlands
Gerrit Rietveld, 1924–1925
Artistic movements can also influence architectural form. The De Stijl (the style) movement in The Netherlands strongly influenced the development of Gerrit Rietveld's architecture, in particular his Schröder House in Utrecht.

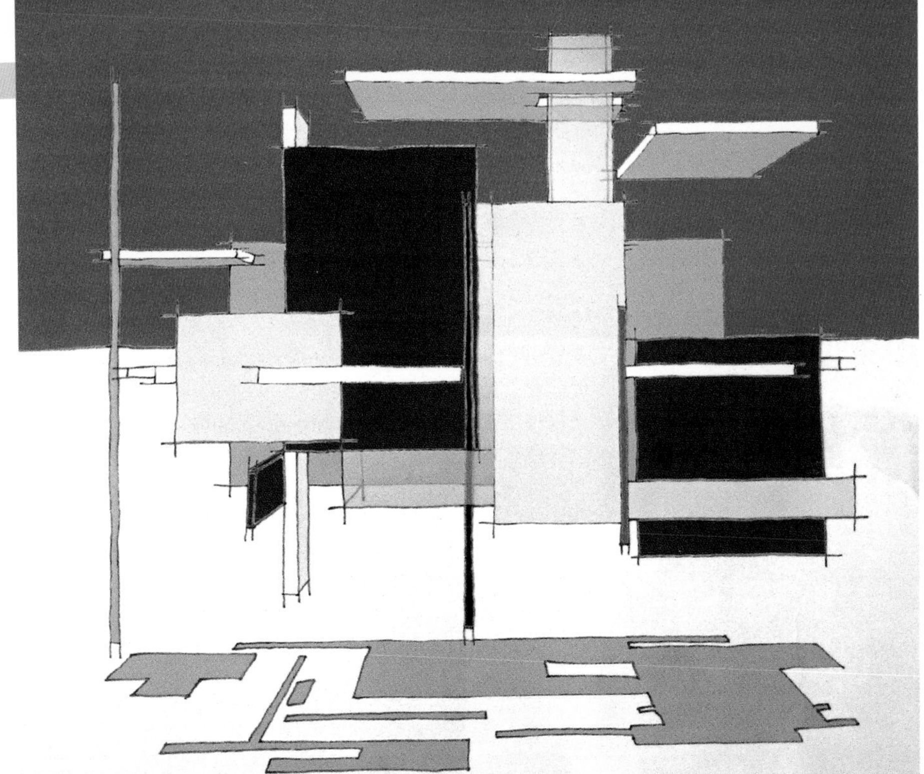

Architecture can also have spiritual associations or connections; these might be reflected in the way that light moves within a particular room, or how the materials used respond to touch. A finished building is a complete sensory experience. Some of these experiences will have been designed, while others are unpredictable and emotional, created through human engagement with the architecture.

Architecture needs to be considered at a range of scales, intensities and levels to develop and evolve. This book will introduce the fundamental principles and explain their relevance to the expression and development of a piece of architecture. Visual language is an essential method of expression for all architects. In this book you will have an introduction to as many of these methods of expression as possible so that you can engage in the exciting world of architecture.

4. Analysis of the Schröder House
This three-dimensional perspective drawing of the Schröder House suggests how the internal spaces of the building are defined by intersecting horizontal and vertical planes. The shadow projected at the bottom of the drawing directly connects to the building's plan.

Chapter 1
Placing Architecture

In architectural terms, 'context' generally refers to the place in which architecture or buildings are located. Context is specific and significantly affects how an architectural idea is generated. Many architects use context to provide clear connection with their architectural concept, so the resultant building is integrated and almost camouflaged as part of its environment. Other responses may react against the environment, and the resultant buildings will be clearly distinct and separate from their surroundings. Either way, the critical issue is that the context has been studied, analysed and responded to deliberately and clearly.

1. dRMM
Model Showing Mixed use Development in Liverpool, 2005
This urban scale model shows the context of a design project in Liverpool, UK. The proposed building is quite distinctively modelled and can be clearly identified from the existing surrounding site.

Site

Architecture belongs somewhere, it will rest on a particular place: a site. The site will have distinguishing characteristics in terms of topography, location and historical definitions.

UNDERSTANDING SITE

An urban site will have a physical history that will inform the architectural concept. There will be memories and traces of other buildings on the site, and surrounding buildings that have their own important characteristics; from use of materials, or their form and height, to the type of details and physical characteristics that the user will engage with. A landscape site may have a less obvious history. However, its physical qualities, its topography, geology and plant life for example, will serve as indicators for architectural design.

There is a fundamental need for an architect to understand the site that a building sits on. The site will suggest a series of parameters that will affect the architectural design. For example, broad considerations might include orientation (how the sun moves around the site) and access (How do you arrive at the site? What is the journey from and to the building?). Specific considerations could be the nature of the adjacent buildings, their height and mass and the materials used to construct them.

The location of a building relates not only to its site, but also to the area around it. This presents a further range of issues to be considered, such as the scale of surrounding buildings and the materials of the area that have been previously used to construct buildings.

On site it is important to imagine ideas of form, mass, materials, entrance and view. The site is both a limitation to design and provider of incredible opportunities. It is what makes the architecture specific and unique as no two sites are exactly the same. Every site has its own lifecycle, which creates yet more variables in terms of its interpretation and understanding. Site analysis is critical for architecture as it provides criteria for the architect to work with.

2

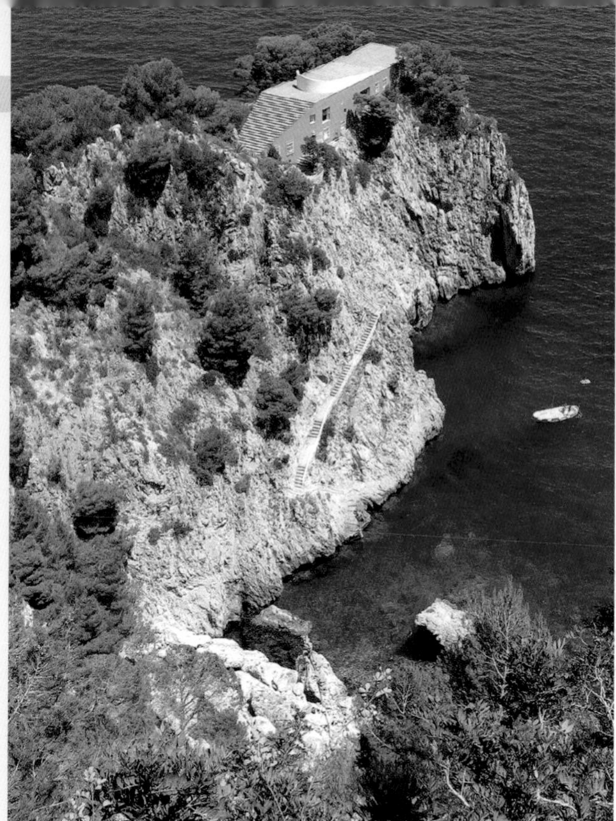

2. Casa Malaparte (Villa Malaparte), Capri, Italy
Adalberto Libera, 1938–1943

Aldalberto Libera provides us with a clear example of a building responding to its landscape. The Casa Malaparte sits on top of a rocky outcrop on the eastern side of the Island of Capri in Italy. It is constructed from masonry, and is so intrinsically connected to its site that it actually appears to be part of the landscape.

3. The London Skyline

In an urban environment, a mixture of historical and contemporary buildings can work well together. The London skyline, viewed from the South Bank, shows a city that has evolved over hundreds of years, each element connecting to the other in terms of material, form and scale.

3

4

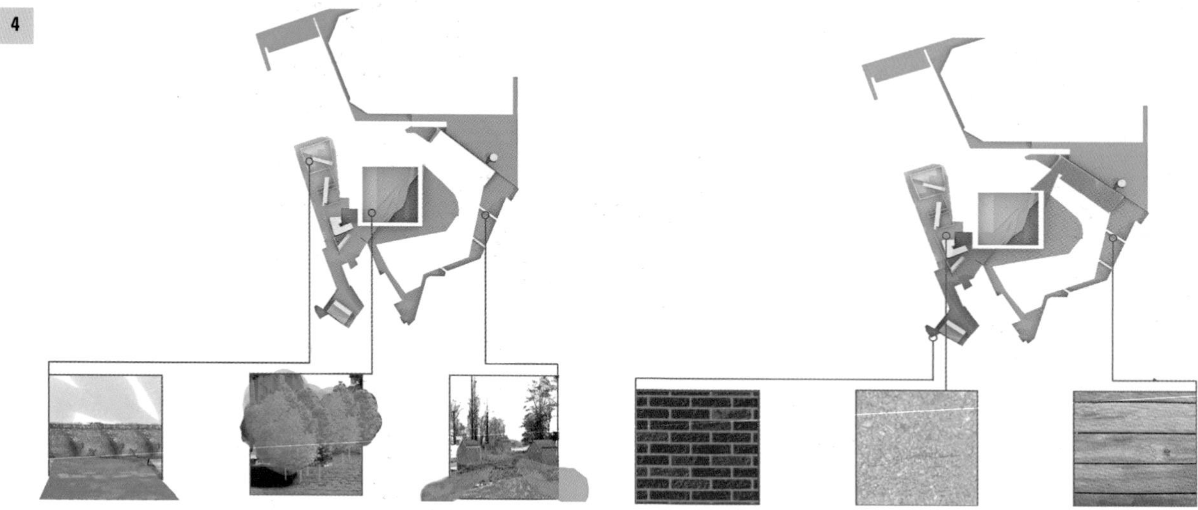

SITE ANALYSIS AND MAPPING

Techniques to record and understand a site are varied, from physical surveys (measuring quantitatively what is there) to qualitatively interpreting aspects of light, sound and experience. Most simply, just to visit a site and watch and record the lifecycle of it can provide clues about how to produce a suitable design response.

Contextual site responses respect the known parameters of the site. Acontextual responses deliberately work against the same parameters to create contrast and reaction. For either approach it is necessary for the architect to have read the site, and properly understood it via various forms of site analysis.

To properly analyse a site it must be mapped, which means recording the many forms of information that exist on it. The mapping needs to include physical aspects of the site, but also more qualitative aspects of the experience and personal interpretations of the place.

There are a range of tools that can be used to map a site, investigate it and produce a design from its indicators. These are analytical tools that allow the site to be measured in a range of different ways.

5

5. This infamous street I found attractive because of it's simplicity.
6. All trees I noticed in Paris are trimmed very neatly. There is a distinct order in this city.
5
1. Etched glass contrasts with stone gives a good effect.
2. Le centre Pompidou has it skeleton on the outside and it's huge scale is shown here.
7. These stainless steel balls move occasionally and are a piece of modern art, placed in a classical environment.
8. These corinthian columns were owned by the French Royal Family, to enhance their greatness.
3
6
8
3. The glass pyramids at Le Louvre contrast dramastically to the classical architecture.
4. Flying buttresses are a dominant feature of many cathedrals in Paris.
7
4

TOOL ONE: PERSONAL INTERPRETATION OF A SITE

The first impression we have of a place is critical. Our personal interpretations of the overall character of a site will inform subsequent design decisions, and it is important to record these honestly and immediately.

The idea of a personal journey around a site and the interpretation of it is something that Gordon Cullen focuses upon when he describes the concept of 'serial vision' in his book *Concise Townscape*. This concept suggests that the area under study is drawn as a map, and a series of points are then identified on it, each one indicating a different view of the site. These views are then sketched out as small thumbnails, which offer personal impressions of the site's space.

Serial vision is a useful technique to apply to any site (or building), in order to explain how it operates spatially and to identify its significance. The visuals can be created either as a series of sketches or as photographs of the journey, as long as they are assembled and read in sequence.

4. Site Analysis
These drawings analyse an urban site in terms of the site's 'plate surface' – the different surface materials – and its 'green typologies' – the different sorts of green spaces. The drawings allow a quick understanding of these elements within the site as a visual map.

5. Personal Interpretations of a Site
A visual travel diary recording a journey around a city can provide a personal interpretation of a site. This sketchbook records a journey around Paris in images and text.

TOOL TWO: FIGURE GROUND STUDY

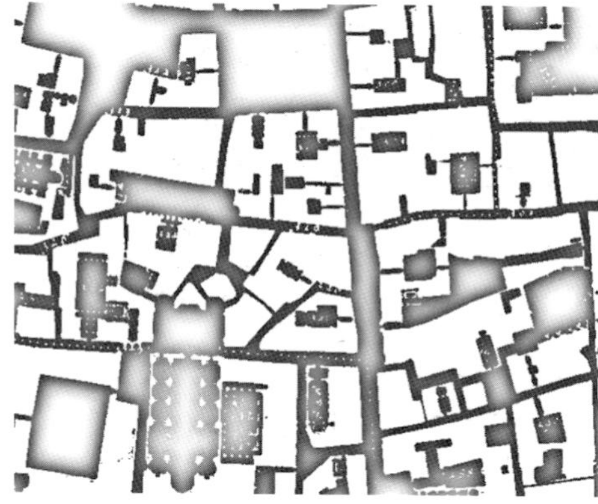

6., 7. & 8. Figure Ground Studies

6. **Nolli's** plan of Rome was initially drawn in 1748 and this interpretation of it shows how spaces can be identified between the buildings. These spaces are read as solid forms, much like a negative for a photograph.
7. Figure ground maps are used to identify a site and distinguish it from its surroundings.
8. This sketch uses figure ground mapping to analyse a site; the building blocks are shaded and the spaces left blank.

A figure ground study is a type of drawing that maps buildings as solid blocks, which then clearly identifies the space around them. A figure ground study presents a city as areas of spaces and solids, producing an abstract site analysis. This exercise allows for a focus on the figure (building) and the ground (space around the building). Historically, figure ground studies have been used to identify the different types of space in cities.

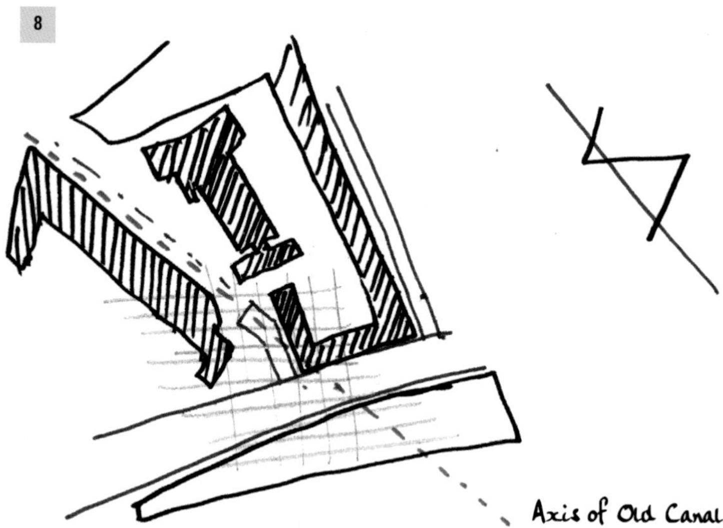

Giambattista Nolli 1701–1756

Nolli was an Italian architect and urban planner. He documented the architecture of Rome and famously produced the city's 'great plan', which detailed the buildings as solids and the spaces between blank. Nolli's great plan reads much like a photographic negative, emphasising the spaces between buildings. It has an additional distinction as it identifies those spaces in the city, the squares, streets and open areas, which are accessible to the public.

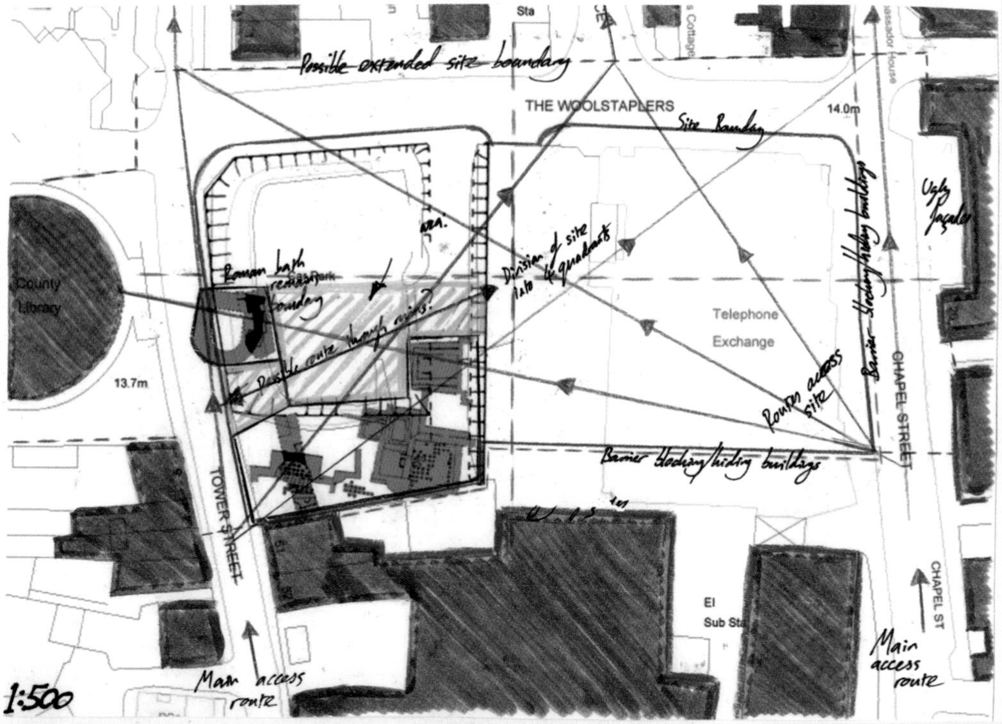

TOOL THREE: HISTORICAL TRACING OF THE SITE

Mapping a site over a series of significant stages in the course of its history provides a description of the life and memory of a place. Historical tracing can be achieved by overlaying a range of same-scale maps from the same site, each one depicting a different stage of the site's development. Doing so allows all the maps to be read concurrently and produces an image of the site that captures both its past and present.

Historical tracing can provide important triggers for a design idea. There may be a historic route, path, road or railway line that could suggest a significant axis, which could be acknowledged in a design idea. Similarly, remains of Roman walls or other important structures could also be recognised in a new building proposal. Historical site analysis can provide inspiration for a contemporary idea that connects directly with past archaeology of a site.

9. Historical Tracing of a Site
Historical site mapping can bring together all the significant developments in a site's lifespan. This provides a 'complete' picture of the site, which can then be used as a source of inspiration for future concepts.

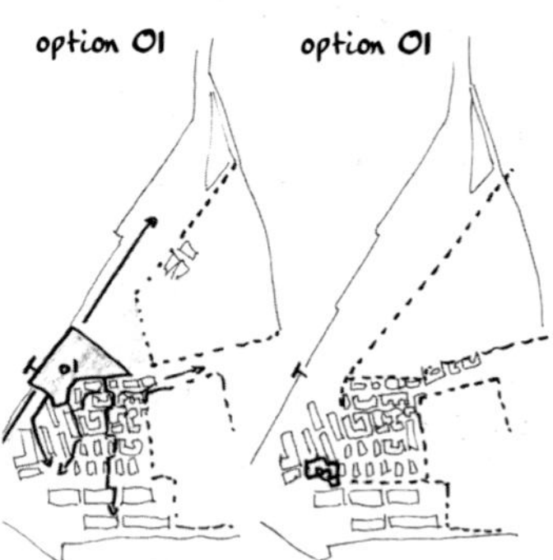

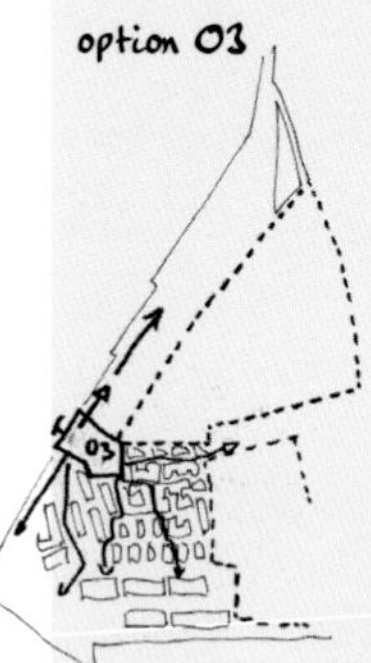

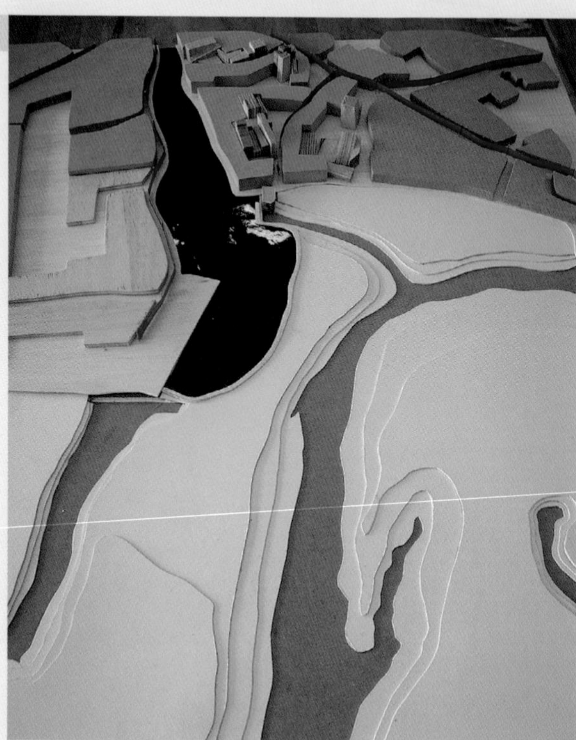

SITE SURVEYS

The condition of any site will need to be recorded in a survey. A survey can be described as a record of something already in existence, and can be produced either in the form of a physical map or model, or a measured drawing that explains where doors, windows or boundaries exists, as well as specific information such as relative heights of surrounding buildings, elevation details or heights of ground level across a site.

Detailed site analysis will measure physical aspects of the site. A site survey will provide dimensions of its width and depth and indicate any adjacent building at the levels of plan, elevation and section (see page 100) to create an accurate record of what currently exists. This is an essential part of the design process.

Site surveys also can record different 'levels'. A level site survey shows the variations of contours and inclines and these may also be used to suggest ways in which to develop the design concept.

10., 11. & 12. Site Surveys
10. This image depicts a series of options for an urban scheme design described as a set of maps.
11. Physical surveys can be in the form of a model or a map. A model can highlight specific characteristics of a site, such as the sea or a river.
12. This analysis of a journey through a city is displayed as a set of overlaid maps and photographic views. The maps are pulled apart and can be read as separate routes and journeys, isolating specific ideas.

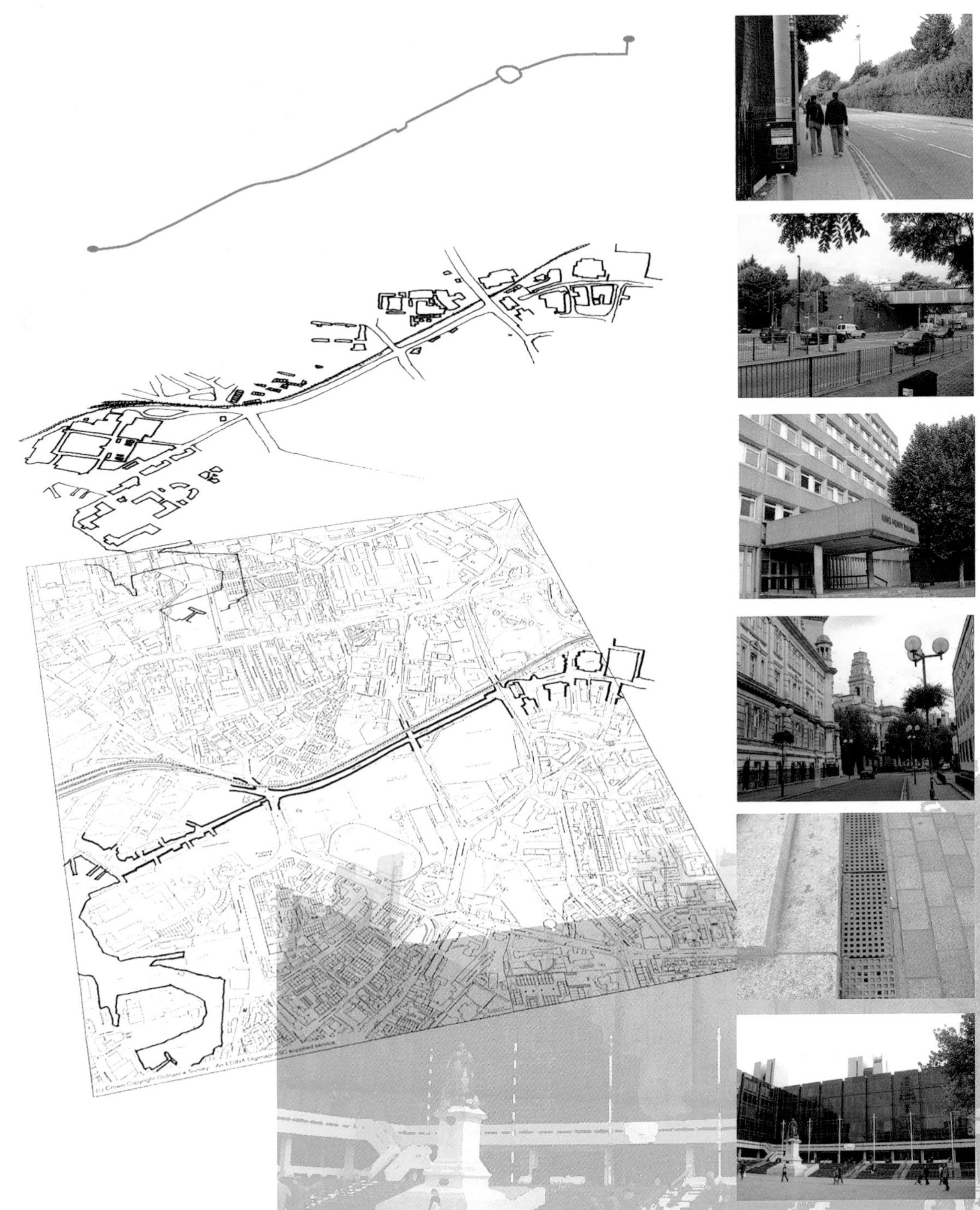

Orientation

In terms of architecture and building, orientation describes an understanding of how a building's position on a site can influence specific factors concerning its design. How light affects our appreciation of buildings, and the activities we experience within them, is one of the most fundamental aspects of architectural design. Natural light in interior space brings life, a moving dimension and a connection with time and the outside.

POSITION

Sites have specific and unique location qualities, and this creates dynamic and ever-changing circumstances for anything positioned on it. For example, the shadow a building projects will change from one day to the next, and the light quality in any room will continually move and change.

The position of a building relative to natural light determines many aspects of its planning. In a house, the position of a garden terrace or the location of, say, a dining room, rely on an architect's understanding of how light enters a room or how shadow is cast across a garden. On larger scale buildings, orientation can significantly affect heat loss in winter and heat gain in summer. This will affect the energy efficiency of the building and the comfort of its users.

The positioning of a building is part of the mechanics of understanding the site, and it provides a changing varying impression of the site, from the point when the sun rises to when it sets, and from the summer solstice (when the sun is at its highest point), to the winter solstice (when it is at its lowest).

Design Orientation Factors

1. For living accommodation in the northern hemisphere, in design terms, bedrooms should be east facing and dining rooms west facing to enjoy the light from the rising and setting sun.
2. South facing buildings will need some form of protection from sunlight. During summer months solar heat gain can raise temperatures to uncomfortable levels. This protection or modification can be in the form of internal blinds or brise soleil (external projections that affect the light entering the building).
3. North light can provide constant and unvarying light.
4. Orientation is concerned with prevailing wind as well as sunlight; different aspects or elevations of buildings may need to be treated in different ways to acknowledge this.
5. Buildings project shadows; understanding orientation requires an appreciation of the potential effect a building mass could have on its site or that of an adjacent one.

13

14

15

16

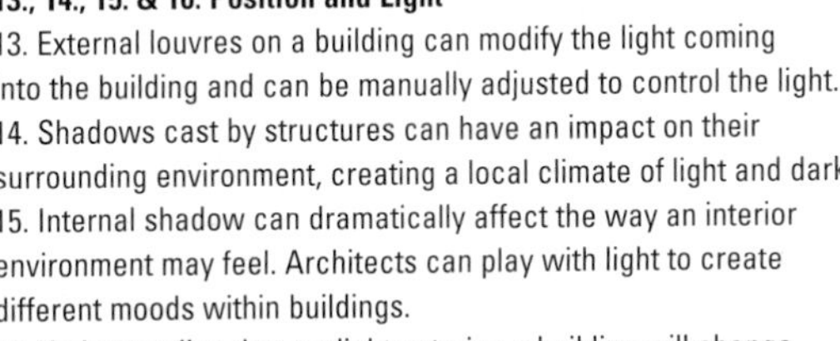

13., 14., 15. & 16. Position and Light

13. External louvres on a building can modify the light coming into the building and can be manually adjusted to control the light.
14. Shadows cast by structures can have an impact on their surrounding environment, creating a local climate of light and dark.
15. Internal shadow can dramatically affect the way an interior environment may feel. Architects can play with light to create different moods within buildings.
16. Understanding that sunlight entering a building will change over the course of the day or will vary from season to season informs the design and layout of the interior spaces.

Climate

Climate is a key contributing factor to the specific nature of site, and climatic variations influence many factors associated with architecture. Buildings will serve as a moderator from the inside to outside.

17

RAINFALL

There are numerous examples of site responses that are driven by climate, perhaps because there is a desire to control or modify it, or perhaps to use local resources that climatic conditions have created.

Climate affects temperature ranges and rainfall. In inclement climates there is clear distinction between the interior and exterior of a building. Rain will need to be prevented from entering buildings and all architecture has to be waterproof. To satisfy this requirement buildings have gutters and pipes and roofs that slope at particular angles to take the rainwater away efficiently and effectively, and these will affect the form and appearance of the architecture.

17. Local Materials
Climate can affect the range of available local materials. This building in the Swiss Alps uses local timber for its structure, and also for its floor and walls.

18. Temperature and Rainfall
A small beach hut offers a minimal separation between the inside and outside. In more extreme temperatures the roof structure is important to provide shelter from the sun.

19. Experimental Pavilion Structure, RWTH University, Aachen, Germany
This open pavilion demonstrates the simplest structure: a roof supported by columns provides basic shelter.

18

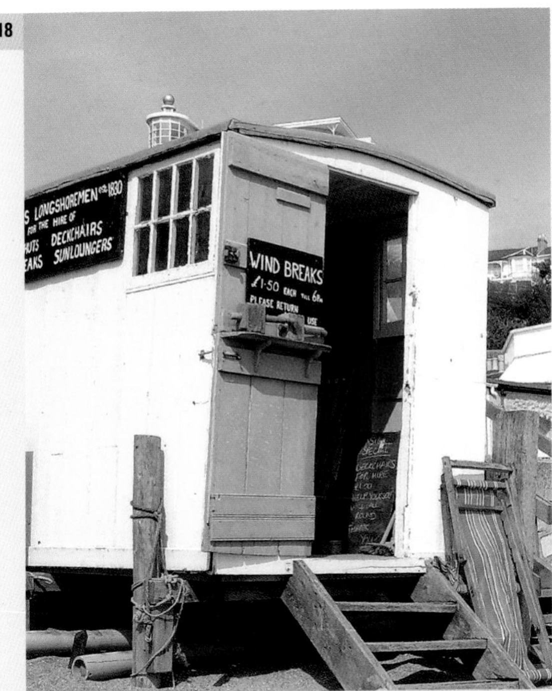

TEMPERATURE

In temperate climates, the inside and outside distinction is much less clear. If there is little rainfall or inclement weather, buildings can be lighter in material terms and buildings can serve as frames that help to define spaces. In this respect architecture is much like a suit of clothes that can be modified according to the external environment and its effects.

Extremes of temperature will affect architectural design requirements in order to ensure that the internal environment is comfortable and habitable. For example, cold weather necessitates thick, insulated walls to keep internal temperatures manageable. Similarly, reducing the glazing used in a building that is located in a very cold climate will reduce the building's heat loss.

Conversely, hot weather requires designs that encourage cooling, use light materials and incorporate features that prevent sunlight heating internal spaces.

In these climates, architectural designs need to encourage cross ventilation in structures to keep the internal temperatures cool. In very hot climates, pools of water can be used to cool spaces and keep the air humid as an effective design solution.

19

Materials

The palette of materials chosen for a building will collectively paint an impression of it. Choosing this palette of materials relies on a clear understanding of the site. Each site, whether urban or landscape, has an intrinsic materiality.

LOCALITY

Historically, the choice of materials at an architect's disposal would have been restricted by local availability and modes of available transportation to the site. Therefore, architecture would have been constructed from materials from the locality, stones sourced from a local quarry, bricks made from local clay, thatch produced from fields surrounding the site and so on. These buildings were literally made from the earth around them and as such they looked like they were part of the landscape of the area. As materials have become more widely available, this palette has expanded.

Materials used in architectural forms no longer have to have this strong connection to their place of origin, they can be moved easily from location to location, resulting in responses that are much more varied and eclectic. The development of materials such as concrete have created endless possibilities in terms of architectural form, as this is a construction material that is universally adaptable and applicable. It has opened up the potential opportunity for ground-breaking architectural design and form making.

20

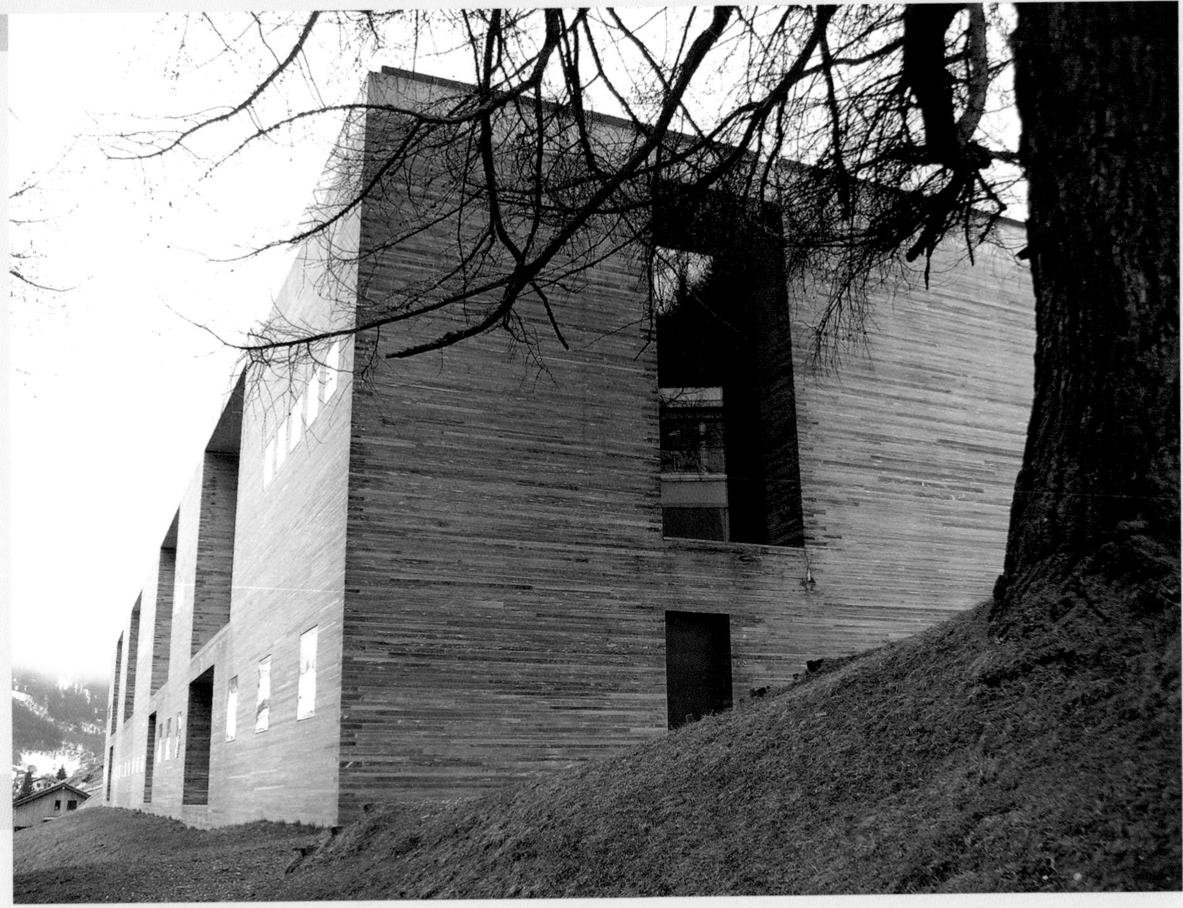

20. Thermal Baths, Vals, Switzerland
Peter Zumthor, 1990–1996
This building sits on a site that has a thermal source of water and has redefined the experience of the thermal baths. It is made from horizontal layers of local Valser quartzite and concrete. Water, light and to some extent steam and heat, add to the definition of areas within the ritual of the bath. The materials used to construct the building connect it to its site and purpose.

Places and Spaces

When does a space become a place? A space is physical, it has dimensions, it is located somewhere, it experiences change through time and it inhabits memory. A place is somewhere that activities, events and occasions happen. A building can be a place or a series of places. A city equally can be made up of many important spaces as well as being a place itself.

THE MEMORY OF PLACE

The concept of memory of place is based on the premise that impressionable places are strongly remembered; they have significant characteristics, sounds, textures, events that make them memorable. For architects, understanding the sense of place is particularly important when responding to, for example, a historic site or a building in a conservation area. There will be aspects of the history and the memory of the site that need to be reinforced.

Designing architecture and cities as places requires an understanding of the events that may take place, as well as the events that have already occurred. There is a need for imagined buildings or spaces that can be considered as arenas for these events to occur.

Carlo Scarpa 1906–1978
An Italian architect, Carlo Scarpa approached historic sites by placing his own contemporary architecture within an existing environment. He did this with great care and deliberation, using a range of forms and materials that are clearly identifiable from the existing building, yet they are still complementary. Scarpa carefully studied his site and respected important aspects of route, movement, view and reinforced these ideas with his own designs. He has respected and explored aspects of the memory of the site.

21. Castelvecchio, Verona, Italy
Restoration by Carlo Scarpa 1954–1967
Castelvecchio (old castle) is a historic Italian castle and Scarpa's restoration transformed it into a relevant, contemporary piece of architecture. It still can be read as a castle, but also as a contemporary sculpture garden and museum.

22. Drawings from Event-Cities (Vol. 1, MIT Press, 1994)
Bernard Tschumi
In his book, 'Event-Cities', Tschumi explores the possibility of a city as a series of potential places for events (such as living, performing, buying or selling), to occur. These maps suggest the physical location of these events.

21

22

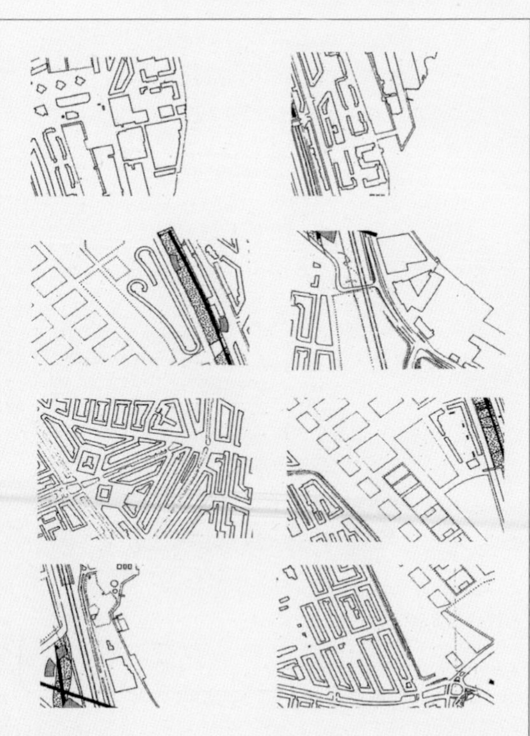

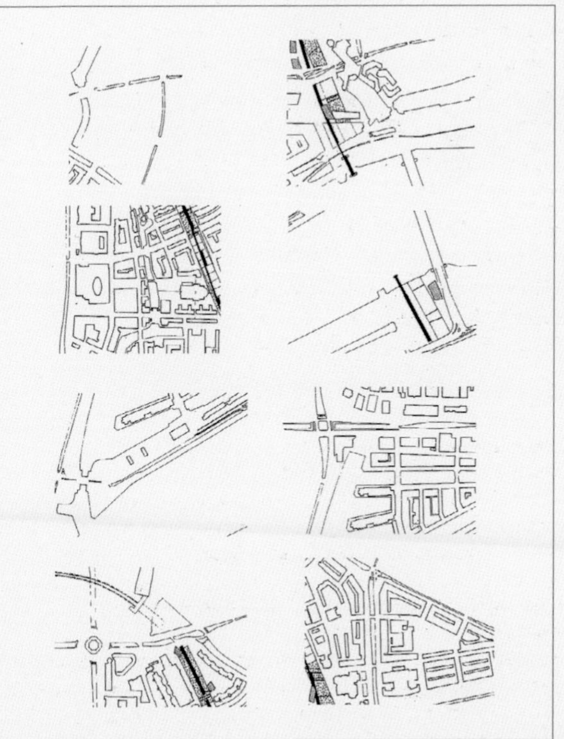

24

Understanding the City

The city is an environment in which much of our new architecture is placed. It is a context for living and working in contemporary society. The city provides precedent for architecture and an environment to interact with and enrich.

Cities are places for events to occur and for life to unfold, they are constructs created by and engaged with thousands of people. Cities are imagined and depicted by many innovators, architects, politicians, artists, authors and designers.

There are many imagined views of the city. Many of these ideas represent a utopia of what a city could be and how we might live our lives. Realisation of these ideals have been seen, to a certain degree, in Seaside in the US, Milton Keynes in the UK and Chandigarh in India. These new cities were first imagined and then created as new and complete concepts for living. Their design was not restricted by issues of historical infrastructure or a limited palette of available materials, instead there was an architectural opportunity to start afresh and build a new future.

23

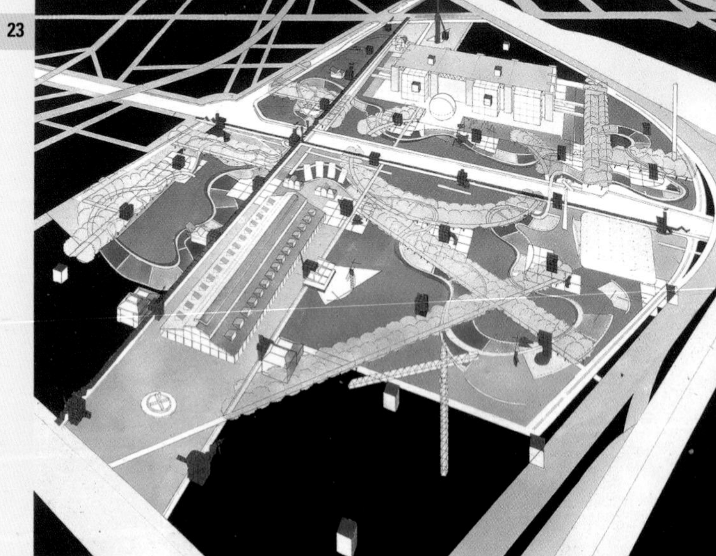

23. Parc de la Villette, Paris, France
Bernard Tschumi, 1982
Tschumi's parc represents a layered scheme. The ground plan denotes the gardens, a series of lines (seen here in both red and blue) shown the paths or routes through the parc and a series of points (shown in red) highlight the follies.

24. Panoramic View of an Urban Scheme
European Cities Studio, 2006
This image suggests an abstract idea of an imagined city. The image shows how the space in a city might be used over a 24-hour period. Although it is a static image, movement is implied via the collage technique used to create the view.

25. Parc de la Villette, Paris, France
Bernard Tschumi, 1982
One of Parc de la Villette's 35 red follies (pavilions), which house cafés, information kiosks and other activity centres.

25

Understanding Landscape

Within the context of landscape, buildings can become part of the environment or distinct and separate from it. Many large buildings or structures can themselves be considered as types of landscape, such as airports, parks or mainline train stations. They are structures so large in scale that they contain buildings and other structures within them.

A landscape, whatever its scale, creates new possibilities for dwelling, inhabiting and living. Whether a site is urban, open, closed or rural, in order for an architect to respond to it with a design proposal it needs to be understood, in both intuitive and personal ways, as well as quantitative and measured means.

Together, these varying aspects of understanding provide important parameters to suggest an architectural solution, one that will be appropriate to the place and its meaning, and contributes something to its context.

26. Madrid Barajas Airport, Madrid, Spain
Richard Rogers Partnership, 1997–2005
Contemporary buildings, such as airports, exist at such a vast scale that they become in themselves a landscape. This RRP designed airport shows the organic form that has been created within a landscape. The building's legible, modular design creates a repeating sequence of waves formed by vast wings of prefabricated steel. Supported on central 'trees', the roof is punctuated by roof lights providing carefully controlled natural light throughout the upper level of the terminal.

Chapter 2
History and Precedent

Design and innovation builds on precedent, on ideas and concepts that have evolved over time. Architecture uses precedents from social and cultural history and applies these influences to contemporary buildings, forms and structures. Having a historical understanding of buildings is an essential part of architectural design because it allows a relationship between the material, physical and formal developments that have been previously explored by other architects. Reacting against, or responding to these ideas has been the basis of architectural evolution.

1

1. Threshold Watercolour Study
Colin Graham, 2002
This watercolour study of a doorway combines a series of section, plan and elevation drawings to reveal the nature of the entrance to this building. Its scale, use of materials and shadow are described effectively with watercolour technique. The entrance way is a combination of arches and uses classical proportions to relate size of doorway, width of arch and depth of colonnade.

3100 BC
Stonehenge in Wiltshire, England, is a monument made of a circle of stones. These sarsen stones weigh up to 50 tonnes each and originated over 50 km away. The structure is aligned with solstice and equinox points and is still used to celebrate these events today.

2600 BC
The pyramids at Giza in Egypt represent the most enduring of architectural symbols. Intended as tombs for the Pharaoh Cheops and his successors, they were built from stone and involved the organisation of several thousand men to construct. The pyramids represent one of the most famous and wondrous monuments in the world.

450 BC
The Acropolis in Athens, Greece, is a collection of buildings constructed on the Acropolis Hill. It consists of the Parthenon, Erectheion and the temple of Nike. They represent the most enduring symbols of classical architecture and culture.

AD 126
The Pantheon was built by Roman emperor Hadrian and intended as a temple for all gods. He used concrete to create an impressive dome structure with an open oculus at the top that allows light to trace across the inner space.

1194
Chartres Cathedral near Paris, France, represents a gothic style of architecture and it achieves an impressive internal nave height of 37 metres. Flying buttresses provide external support on the walls to help achieve this height.

1417
Filippo Brunelleschi was a Florentine architect who famously designed the Duomo in Florence, Italy. Brunelleschi developed a machine to allow perspective to be analysed and drawn. The machine was constructed from a series of mirrors that allowed him to analyse what he saw. Until this point, painting and images did not represent perspective accurately as there was no conceptual or mathematical understanding of it.

1492
Leonardo da Vinci's Vitruvian Man represents the relationship between man and geometry. It was inspired by Da Vinci's studies of Vitruvius who described a set of measurements or modules based on man's proportions and dimensions.

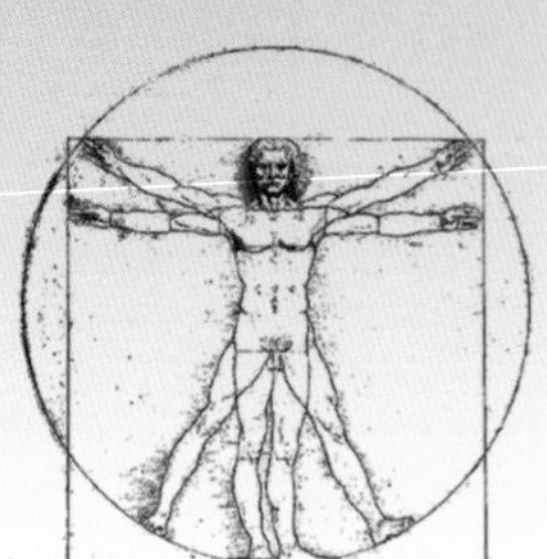

1755
Laugier's hut (or the primitive hut) was described by Abbé Laugier in his seminal essay on architecture. It uses nature to create an analogy with architecture; the trunks of trees form columns, and branches and leaves form the roof. It represents the earliest and simplest form of shelter.

1779
Constructed from cast iron, the Iron Bridge in Shropshire, England, represents the industrial revolution and the new materials and technologies that were to revolutionise building form. Iron was to create the potential for lighter, more ambitious structures and buildings.

1919
The Bauhaus movement began its life as an art and architecture school in Weimar, Germany. It was directed by some of the most influential architects and designers of the twentieth century, including Walter Gropius, Hannes Meyer, Ludwig Mies van der Rohe and László Maholy-Nagy among others.

1851
Joseph Paxton built London's Crystal Palace for the great exhibition of 1851. Paxton introduced a new type of architecture, inspired by technology, engineering and innovation. Combining a lightweight iron frame with glass created a transparent piece of architecture.

1924
Gerrit Rietveld designed the Schröder House in The Netherlands. It is the best-known example of De Stijl architecture and is a building that has no internal walls. The Schröder House was part of a philosophy that simplified visual composition to horizontal elements and use of primary colours and black and white.

1947
Le Corbusier, who was interested in the idea of proportion, geometry and the human body, developed the modulor system. Le Modulor was published and used as a scale to design many buildings including the Ronchamp Chapel in France.

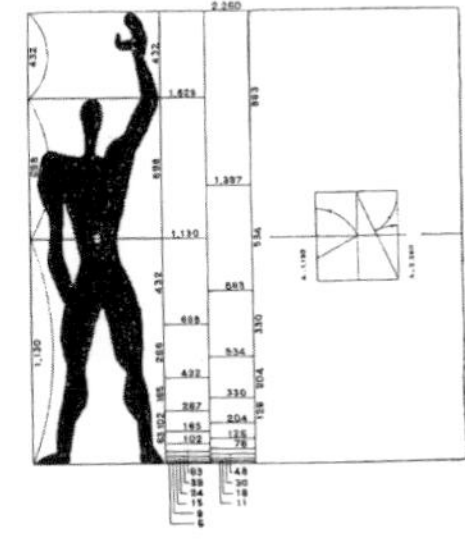

2000
Marks Barfield architects built the London Eye originally as a temporary structure to celebrate the millennium, but it has since become as celebrated a piece of architecture as the Eiffel Tower in Paris. It is a work of engineering and a dynamic piece of urban architecture at the same time, challenging our view of London.

1889
The Eiffel Tower in Paris was built for the Exposition Universelle. Designed by engineer Gustave Eiffel, it was the tallest cast iron frame structure of its time. The tower was originally intended as a temporary structure, but now forms an important part of the city's identity.

1929
The Barcelona Pavilion was designed in 1929 by German architect Ludwig Mies van der Rohe. It represented a new type of modern architecture that questioned the position of walls, floors and roofs, and introduced a new vocabulary of planes and surfaces.

1931
Shreve, Lamb and Harmon designed the Empire State Building in New York. It was the highest frame structure of its time at 102 storeys.

1972
The Pompidou Centre in Paris, designed by Renzo Piano and Richard Rogers, reinvented the idea of the building as a machine. All the services, lifts, pipework and ventilation ducts are placed on the outside of the building for dramatic effect.

2. The Pyramids at Giza, Egypt
c. 2600 BC
Pharoahs saw the building of these tombs as an expression of their reign, much as international corporations and governments of today build taller and more expensive buildings as symbols of their power and importance.

The Ancient World

The history of architecture is intrinsically aligned with the history of civilisation. While our nomadic ancestors had developed sophisticated forms of temporary shelter – some of which are still used today, such as the yurt tents of the peoples of the Mongolian plain – the change to a more sedentary form of existence fuelled the need for permanent shelter.

The first such built forms fulfilled the function of providing shelter from the elements, for example, the first known houses at Çatal Hüyük in Anatolia. They also served to protect property and people through fortifications and to establish cultural identity. Beginning in the fertile alluvial valleys along the rivers Tigers and Euphrates in Mesopotamia, which occupies much of modern-day Iraq, the early Sumerian civilisation produced the origins of much of the architecture that was to follow.

ANCIENT EGYPT

In contrast to the city states of Mesopotamia, which were often warring with each other, the Nile (in its final 1100-km journey to the Mediterranean) was surrounded on either side by desert, and this made assault from the outside more difficult and resulted in a society that remained untainted by external influences for more than 3000 years. During this period the Egyptians developed architecture that was characterised in the early dynastic periods by pyramidal burial tombs formed above ground and, later, by the richly decorated tombs in the Valley of the Kings.

In both instances the buildings reflected the strongly held Egyptian belief in life after death. This belief was mirrored in everyday life too, and experienced as a series of dualities: night and day, flood and drought, water and desert. This belief and such dualities explain why the Valley of the Kings is located on the western side of the Nile, the horizon on which the sun sets, while the temples and settlements of Luxor are on the eastern side, the horizon of the rising sun.

This symbolic positioning of ancient Egyptian buildings was further enhanced by the precision with which they were constructed. The pyramids of Giza were built (around 2600 BC), accurate to 100 mm over their 150-metre perfectly square base, and the apex of the pyramid creates a precise geometric form derived from the golden section (see page 117). Within each pyramid, small passages running from the burial chambers are precisely aligned with celestial constellations, as these were seen as the resting place to which the soul of the pharaohs would travel in the afterlife.

The scale and exactness of execution of these structures is breathtaking, and required, even by today's standards, an enormous feat of engineering, not least in sourcing the several million stone blocks used in their construction. These stones were quarried in Upper Egypt, some 640 km from the site, and were transported by water before being raised into position.

3

NEOLITHIC STRUCTURES

The Stone Age comprises of three periods, Palaeolithic, Mesolithic and Neolithic. Neolithic cultures created great stone structures in the landscape of the British Isles. Often forming large stone circles, these structures are impressive due to their scale, method of construction and the connections that they appear to have with the tracks in the sky of the sun and moon. The most impressive Neolithic structures can be found in Wiltshire, England, the Orkney Isles and in Ireland, both in the east at Newgrange and in the west in the Aran Islands.

Stonehenge, however, is probably the most well-known Neolithic structure. The stone circle formation on this site dates from around 3100 BC. Initially Stonehenge was a series of holes, commonly described as an 'earthwork'. This was superseded a thousand years later by the next stage of construction, which involved transporting the stones. To get the stone to the site it had to be loaded onto rafts and carried by water from the southwest coast of Wales, along the rivers Frome and Avon and eventually across land to its resting place on Salisbury plain. The next stage was the arrival of the sarsen stones (the largest of which weighed around 50 tonnes); these were transported from Marlborough Downs near Avebury in north Wiltshire, about 40 km north of Stonehenge.

Stonehenge was not built out of necessity. It is not a construction concerned with shelter, but instead represents a spiritual connection with the natural and celestial worlds.

4

3. Stonehenge, Wiltshire, UK
c. 3100–2000 BC

Stonehenge is a Neolithic and Bronze Age megalithic monument. It is composed of earthworks surrounding a circular setting of large standing stones and is one of the most famous prehistoric sites in the world. Archaeologists think that the standing stones were erected between 2500 BC and 2000 BC although the surrounding circular earth bank and ditch have been dated to about 3100 BC.

4. Newgrange Megalithic Tomb, Knowth, Ireland
c. 3200 BC

This is the oldest solar conservatory in the world. At a width of more than 80 metres, Newgrange is a vast mound of rocks, stones and earth. It has remained intact for 5000 years. It was built to celebrate the winter solstice sunrise during which a shaft of light enters the heart of the tomb and illuminates its inner chamber.

The Classical World

In architecture, the influence of Roman and Greek civilisations is found in the concepts, forms, ideas, decorations and proportions that have been reinterpreted as renaissance (in fifteenth-century Italy), Georgian (in nineteenth-century London) and American colonial styles. There is an enduring sense of elegance and balance to classical architecture and ideas.

ANCIENT GREECE

While the civilisations of Mesopotamia and Egypt formed the foundations of architecture, it was in the societies of ancient Greece that the language of the discipline was first formalised.

Much of our modern culture finds its origins in the civilisation of classical Greece. Political democracy, theatre and philosophy derive from a society that, having mastered the supply of food, found they had spare time to think, reflect and better understand the rules of the world around them. Some of the greatest minds in history, Plato, Aristotle and Pythagoras, laid down the patterns of thinking that would dominate western culture for the next 2000 years.

The Hellenistic architecture of ancient Greece (produced during what is described as the 'golden period'), reached such refinement and quality that it subsequently earned its definition of 'classical'.

Today, reference to the classical language of architecture alludes not only to the form, but also to the way in which the architects of ancient Greece developed an architectural methodology that could be applied to all building types.

The literal building blocks of this methodology are the columns used to support the construction. These columns are in one of five forms, according to the slenderness and embellishment of their design. These forms are: Tuscan, Doric, Ionic, Corinthian and Composite, and rank in order from short and squat to slender and elegant. Collectively they are known as the five orders.

The diameter of each column not only determined its height, but also the space allowed between columns and therefore the overall ratio and proportions of the building it was supporting. Each individual element of Greek architecture had a mathematical relationship to every other element, making the building an integrated totality.

5. The Five Orders of Classical Architecture
The public buildings of the ancient Greeks and Romans were almost all designed using the five 'orders' of architecture. The orders are expressed according to the design of the column and the details of the upper parts of the façades carried by each. The five orders are: Tuscan, Doric, Ionic, Corinthian and Composite, and their designs range from simple and unadorned to highly decorative. The numbers in this diagram refer to the column's height/diameter ratio. For example, the Tuscan column's height is seven times its diameter.

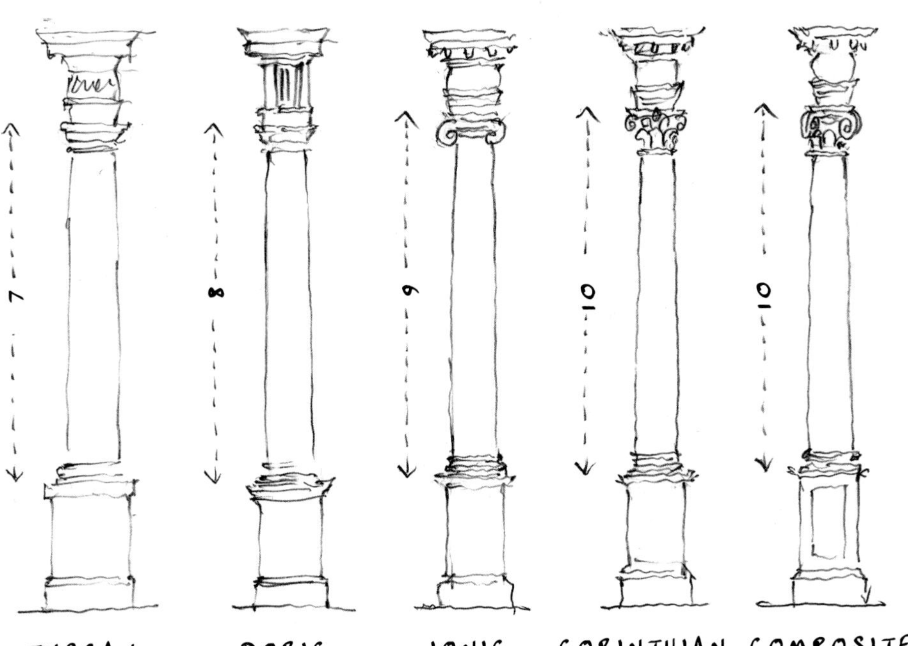

This modular system, where the width of the column determined the proportions of the building, created a formula for design. This blueprint could be equally applied to a small house or a whole city and in so doing a connected and harmonious architecture could be created.

Many examples of Ancient Greek classical architecture remain, and perhaps the best known is the Acropolis in Athens; the symbolic centre of the classical world. The Acropolis is effectively a fortified collection of individual buildings centred on the great temple of the Parthenon. This architectural icon was a place of worship housing a giant (16-metre) ivory and gold covered statue of the goddess Athene, patron of the city. Although few had the privilege to view the statue, the building's exterior was an expression of civic and national pride.

Its frieze, the band of sculpted panels that surrounded the building above the column line, is considered to contain some of the finest works of art ever made. The subject of much controversy, they are now housed in the British Museum and depict the Great Panathen, the four-yearly ritual robing of the Athene, with such lifelike execution that solid marble seems to flow in the folds of material in the gods' gowns. This highlights the value that the Greeks placed in observation and understanding of the human form.

The classical world also devised urban planning. In cities such as Miletus and Priene, the social order was reflected in their houses and focal public buildings, assembly halls and gymnasia, which were all carefully laid out on a grid plan. Above all, their urban planning focused on the interchange of goods and ideas, and the 'agora' or marketplace might be considered the public heart of the Greek city.

In addition, the architects of Ancient Greece produced great amphitheatres, able to accommodate an audience of 5000 with ease, providing perfect sight lines and acoustics, qualities that many architects find it hard to emulate today.

6. **The Colosseum, Rome, Italy**
AD c. 72–82
The Colosseum is a giant amphitheatre in the centre of Rome. Originally capable of seating 50,000 spectators, it was used for gladiatorial contests and public spectacles. Although it is now in a severely ruined condition, the Colosseum has long been seen as an iconic symbol of Imperial Rome and is one of the finest surviving examples of Roman architecture.

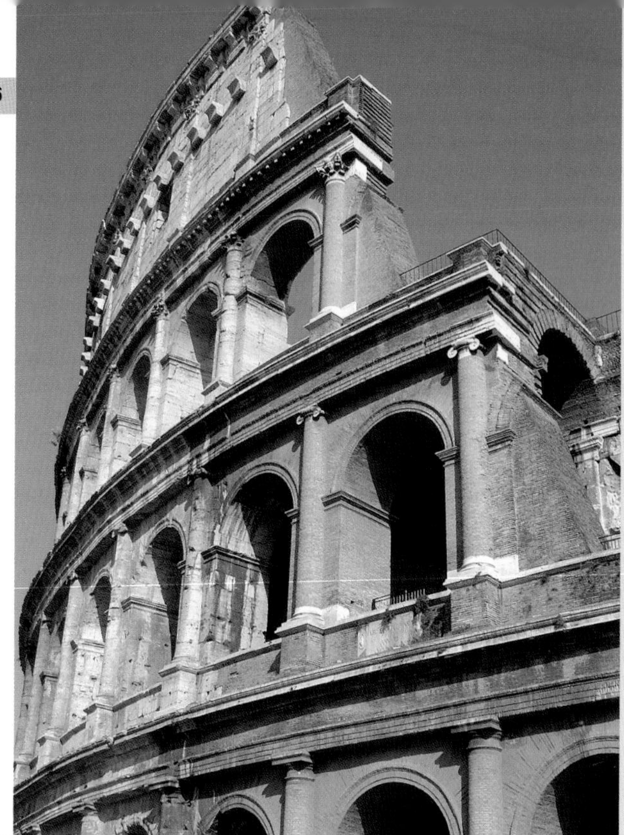
6

ROME

Architecture is perhaps, above all else, a practical concern, and the concept of buildings as works of engineering formed the underlying principle of Roman architecture. Adopting the classical language of Ancient Greece, the Romans, rather than innovating, refined their buildings and construction techniques. Of these methods, the arch is the legacy of Rome to the history of architecture.

Ancient Greece had largely limited much of its architecture to a series of columns connected together by lintels to support a pitched roof. This system restricted the forms that buildings could adopt as their proportions were determined by the maximum span of the horizontal modules. The development of the arch enabled greater spans and curves in plan to be realised. Also far greater loads could be transferred, enabling much larger and less orthogonal structures to be achieved. Some of the first examples of these structures, the Colosseum and the Pantheon, although decorated with classical columns, owe their vast scale to the arch, which underpins their structure.

7. Pantheon (interior), Rome, Italy
AD c. 118–126

The Pantheon is one of the great spiritual buildings of the world. It was originally built as a Roman temple and was later consecrated as a Catholic Church. It has a central opening or oculus that allows light to travel through the building creating a sense of depth on the coffered ceiling. The roof is a dome sitting on top of a simple plan.

7

The Medieval World

The fall of Rome and the descent of western civilisation into the cultural chaos that characterised the Dark Ages prompted a very different view of architecture from that which had existed in the classical world. In times of uncertainty, unsure as to his own abilities to understand the world around him, man often turns to external sources to govern the future. For this reason the medieval period saw a turn away from the secular towards the divine as a source of certainty.

GOTHIC ARCHITECTURE

The primary purpose of much medieval architecture was to communicate the biblical narratives to the largely illiterate masses. To serve this purpose, medieval cathedrals developed a unique form that reduced structural mass and allowed stained glass to illuminate the interior with the divine light and message of a Christian God.

In addition to this, the desire to escape the torments of earthly existence and seek solace in a heavenly realm brought about an emphasis on the vertical, resulting in an architectural style of ascension. Directing the eye heavenward, the Gothic style characteristically employed pointed arches and placed structure outside of the building. A great example of this is to be found in St Chappelle, close to the other great gothic cathedral of Notre Dame, on the Isle de la Cité in Paris, France. A vertical architectural emphasis is seen on its exterior with towering spires that once served as pilgrimage beacons (reflecting the belief that the taller the spire the greater the city's piety).

Gothic architecture also adopted a very precise and often complex geometric organisation where sacred ratios, echoed in the natural world, were employed as a celebration of the divine mind.

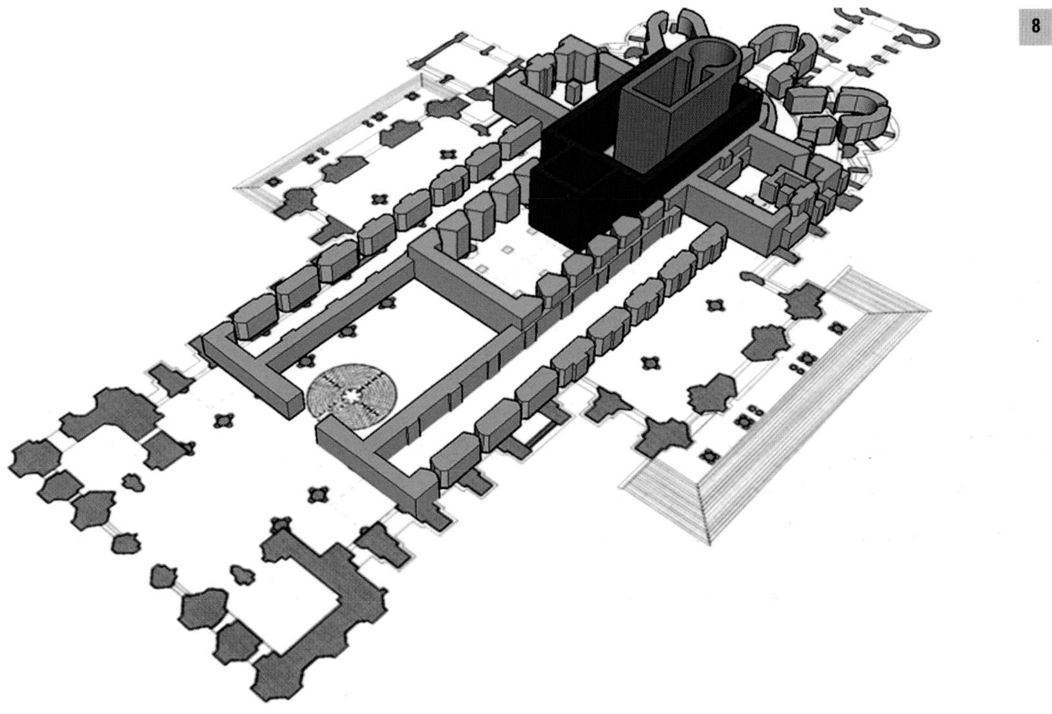

8

In domestic structures the heights of the classical world were lost and Gothic architecture regressed to a largely vernacular type, using local ideas and materials and often based on timber frame construction. While primitive in many respects, the overall results of the construction methods employed by medieval carpenters were of considerable technological ingenuity. The use of local materials in much of their natural form gave the buildings an intimate connection with their regional landscape and location. This is a characteristic that has recently been reinterpreted by the 'green' architecture movement.

In addition to this, the piecemeal development of towns and cities through the period produced irregular urban planning, which gave many towns a certain charm and sense of character. Towards the end of the medieval period, the re-emergence of secular concerns gave rise to more substantial structures based around trading activities. At the smallest scale, this was evident in the many market crosses erected in provincial towns, and at the other end of the spectrum, saw the construction of some of the finest medieval structures, including the Doge's Palace in Venice, Italy, which was one of the few secular constructions crafted to the level of a medieval cathedral.

8. Chartres Cathedral Historical Development
Emma Liddell, 2007
This diagram demonstrates how Chartres Cathedral has evolved from the construction of its early Gallo-Roman inner chapel (dated AD c.500), to the Gothic cathedral (dated AD c.1260) that we are all familiar with. Each new phase of building wraps around the previous one.

The Renaissance

Few times in the history of architecture show the sort of rapid and fundamental changes in attitude as was witnessed in Italy at the beginning of the fourteenth century.

HUMANISM

This period saw a rejection of medieval scholasticism and a revived interest in classical architecture. Those architects who had known Gothic building in Europe, but vividly remembered the great architecture of the Roman Empire, began to reconsider the classical language of architecture. This line of inquiry gathered pace in Florence where wealthy, self-confident merchants and new banking families such as the Medici became patrons to a small group of architects who had started to revalue and tentatively experiment with the classical language of architecture.

To a previous generation, the works of the ancient classical world had seemed a form and complexity beyond experience. The new sensibility sought to understand classical architecture based on the validity of man's reasoning power and his ability to understand the world through observations and intellect rather than any preordained explanation.

Filippo Brunelleschi 1377–1446

Brunelleschi was born in Florence, Italy. Initially trained as a sculptor, he then studied sculpture and architecture in Rome with Donatello. In 1418 Brunelleschi won a competition to design the Duomo of the Santa Maria del Fiore in Florence. His design was the largest dome over the greatest span of its time. Brunelleschi's duomo is made up of a series of layered domes and the space between each is large enough to walk through. He was also responsible for inventing machines to assist with various aspects of architecture, from raising large weights to a better understanding of perspective.

10

Leon Battista Alberti championed this intellectual approach and set out the new discoveries of the classical world in his treatise *De Re Aedificatoria*. In this he promoted the mathematical perfection of platonic forms as a mirror of God's divine perfection, and proposed that a centrally and symmetrically planned church would be more ideal than the familiar form of the Latin cross adopted in Gothic architecture. This ideal was only to take form some years later with Michelangelo's plans for St. Peter's Basilica in Rome, which was testament to the power of Alberti's theoretical writing in architecture.

Perhaps one of the most potent symbols of the Italian renaissance was **Filippo Brunelleschi's** dome of the Santa Maria del Fiore, in Florence; the *duomo*. Here the problem of spanning a 42-metre wide crossing required a solution for which history offered no precedents and Brunelleschi devised an ingenious method of banding the base of the dome with a giant iron chain in order to resist huge outward forces. Brunelleschi adapted the language of the Gothic church plan to produce a semi-circular arcade that was supported on classical columns at Santo Spirito, and used a similar form for the extraordinarily delicate arcade fronting the Foundlings Hospital in London. In this way he reinterpreted the classical language ingeniously and adapted and modified the precedents he found in classical architecture to contemporary building typologies.

9. Santa Maria del Fiore (The Duomo), Florence, Italy
Filippo Brunelleschi, 1417–1434
This octagonal dome dominates the Santa Maria del Fiore. Brunelleschi drew his inspiration from the double-walled cupola of the Pantheon in Rome. The distinctive octagonal design of the double-walled dome, resting on a drum and not on the roof itself, allowed for the entire dome to be built without the need for scaffolding from the ground. This enormous construction weighs 37,000 tonnes and contains over four million bricks.

10. Façade of the Basilica di Santa Maria Novella, Florence, Italy
Completed by Leon Battista Alberti, 1456–1470
This building is unique because all its dimensions are bound to each other by the ratio of 1:2.

11

11. Piazza del Campidoglio, Rome, Italy
Buonarroti Michelangelo, 1538–1650
This space is designed as an elliptical courtyard. Michelangelo also designed the two buildings flanking the piazza to create a sense of increased perspective, exaggerating views across the city. The Piazza del Campidoglio has a centrepiece statue of the Roman emperor Marcus Aurelius. Michelangelo's piazza brings together geometry, route and monument in a coherent piece of urban design.

As the Italian renaissance developed, so the confidence of architects in their own creative powers grew. The late or high renaissance saw Georgio Vasari's *The Lives of the Artists* published, which promoted the idea of the architect as a creative genius, an individual singled out for special powers beyond and above others.

Michelangelo felt that he had such creative powers and looked into his own imagination rather than drawing on outside precedents for inspiration. In so doing he was able to understand the classical language with a unique insight, which enabled him to both master and break its given rules. This is nowhere more evident than in his great entrance vestibule and staircase to the Laurentian Library in Florence.

Here Michelangelo questioned ideas that had previously been used in a very specific way in architecture. Not only did he split the pedimented entrance portal, thus questioning its historic structural role, but he also inverted the columns and cut them out of the wall.

Michelangelo moved architecture more towards the ornamental or illusory; his work was designed to evoke emotions and a feeling of theatricality. During this period the rebirth of classical architecture adopted mannerism (a style that was characterised by distortions in scale and perspective as well as a use of bright colour), and ultimately moved towards the opulence and decadence of the Rococo, with buildings and civic spaces described as theatrical backdrops to the events of the city. This shift is no more evident than in Michelangelo's remodelling of the Capitoline Hill in Rome, which challenged the accepted rules of perspective and introduced buildings with competing elements of various scales within the same composition.

The Baroque and the Enlightenment

The beginning of the eighteenth century witnessed a new age of reasoning. Copernicus, Kepler and Galileo overturned the established geocentric Christian cosmology and asked that if the earth and man were no longer at the centre of the universe, then what other established beliefs could be brought into doubt? This notion was met with an enormous burst of intellectual inquiry, which sought to establish the new rules that would govern what was increasingly considered to be a 'clockwork' universe.

Claude Nicholas Ledoux 1736–1806
Ledoux was a French neoclassical (employing the original classical style from Greece and Rome) architect. He was involved in many monumental and visionary projects such as the Royal Saltworks at Arc-et-Senans in France and the theatre of Besançon in France. Influenced by Greek classical architecture, Ledoux had ideas for a utopian city for a new society.

Etienne-Louis Boullée 1728–1799
Born in Paris, Boullée was involved in many of the city's large-scale symbolic buildings including the national library. He also designed visionary structures that were never realised including the Cenotaph dedicated to Newton, which was a complete spherical structure. Boullée also wrote the influential essay on the art of architecture, which promoted neoclassical architecture.

12

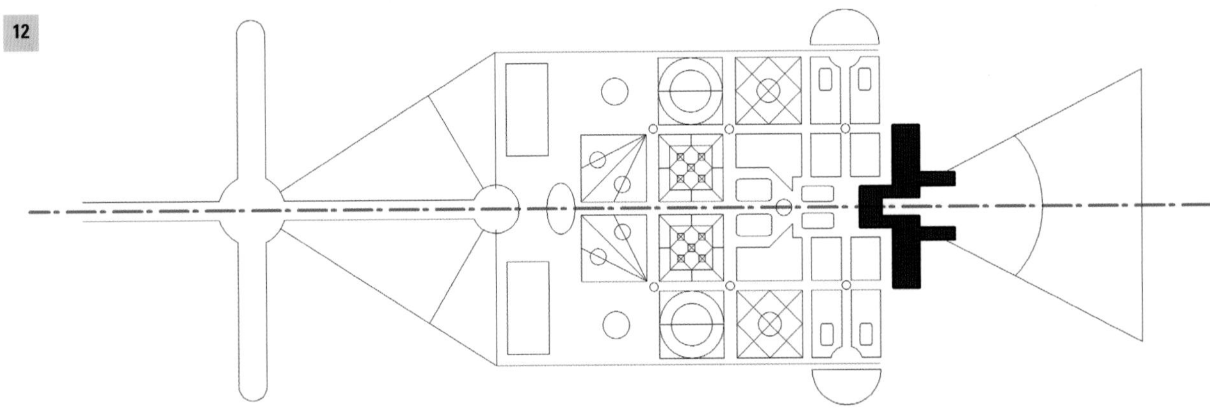

RATIONAL BUILDING

Architecture too followed this pattern of inquiry with theorists such as Abbé Laugier seeking to establish the fundamental principles of the discipline by reducing the essence of building down to a primitive aedicule structure that, by extension, could be universally applied.

In practice architects such as **Ledoux** and **Boullée** devised an architecture of purity that strived for the external truth of form. So-called rational building, derived from the rational philosophy of René Descartes, sought to build on the foundations of logical and deductive reason to produce an architecture based on indubitable premise. Boullée's proposals were of a giant scale and he built very little, but of those he did realise, his monuments to Sir Isaac Newton stand as a symbol of the age. Similarly, Ledoux's barrier gates for the city of Paris and his design for a radial city at Arc-et-Senans pre-empted much of the rational urban planning that would determine the future design of cities.

12. Symmetrical and Rational Plan of the Château de Versailles
This diagram shows the connection, along a central axis, between the gardens and the building of the Château de Versailles. Both plans are symmetrical along the axis. The château was designed by the architect Louis Le Vau and the gardens by landscape architect André Le Notre in 1661.

13. The Château de Versailles, Paris, France
Louis Le Vau, 1661–1774
Initially a small hunting lodge, The Palace of Versailles was extended by successive kings of France and designed to resemble its current form by Le Vau in 1661. It has been designed by architects and landscape architects and is an impressive connection of building and landscape, interior and exterior linked by carefully considered views and axis.

Inigo Jones 1573–1652
Born in England, Jones first studied classical architecture and then travelled to Italy. Heavily influenced by Palladio, who in the sixteenth century had interpreted original classical architecture in his 'Four Books of Architecture' (1570), Jones developed a Palladian style, which was an interpretation of classical architecture.

In England his most influential buildings are the Queen's House at Greenwich, the Banqueting House at Whitehall and the design of Covent Garden in London.

Sir Christopher Wren 1632–1723
Wren studied both astronomy and architecture at Oxford University. The Great Fire of London in 1666 gave him the opportunity to be involved in the rebuilding of the city.

He designed St Paul's Cathedral in London, was involved in the rebuilding of 51 of the city's churches and also designed Hampton Court Palace and Greenwich Hospital.

Nicholas Hawksmoor 1661–1736
Hawksmoor worked alongside Wren on St Paul's Cathedral, Hampton Court and Greenwich Hospital. He also assisted Vanbrugh on Blenheim Palace and Castle Howard.

Hawksmoor adopted the classical style and interpreted it to produce his own approach.

Rational building as a classical form reached the United Kingdom through the work of Inigo Jones, and the political revolutions that followed this intellectual revolution were bought into sharp focus outside the doors of Inigo Jones's Banqueting House with the decapitation of Charles I.

Sir Christopher Wren remodelled much of London following the Great Fire of 1666 in this new enlightened fashion. The dome of St Paul's Cathedral and the surrounding spires by Nicholas Hawksmoor stood like beacons of intellectual clarity against the ramshackle irrational collection of timber-frame buildings that had characterised medieval London. Rational architecture brought a new scale and elegance to the city.

14

14. St Paul's Cathedral, London, UK
Sir Christopher Wren, 1675–1710
This current cathedral was constructed after its predecessor was destroyed by the great fire of London. The dome of St Paul's has a great physical presence on the skyline of London,and is an important visual feature and reference for the city.

However, as the eighteenth century unfolded, the rise of empirical philosophy in the United Kingdom brought an architecture that was the opposite of rational. The notion that truth was to be found through the senses (rather than through intellect) led to the first true landscape design of environments that were devoted to sensory excitation. **Lancelot 'Capability' Brown** devised gardens based on intrigue, variety and contrast, and Henry Hoare's gardens at Stourhead most vividly capture this concept.

Lancelot 'Capability' Brown
1716–1783
Lancelot 'Capability' Brown was an influential British landscape architect who worked on many important eighteenth-century country houses aiming to complement their architecture through his landscape proposals. Brown began his career at Stowe in Buckinghamshire, and his work includes the gardens and estates of Blenheim Palace in Oxfordshire. His approach was to create a complete classical environment comprising a new landscape, lawn, trees, lakes and temples. The result was an illusion of a natural landscape, yet it was totally contrived as each piece had been carefully considered and placed.

15. Stourhead Garden, Wiltshire, UK
Henry Hoare II, 1741–1765
The design of the gardens at Stourhead is a stark contrast to the French ordered style that favours an axis for views and paths. Hoare's approach was to celebrate nature, and the Stourhead gardens are a contrived artificial landscape that makes use of meandering paths to provide glimpses of important features such as the grottoes and follies contained within it.

Modernism

The beginning of the Enlightenment had been accompanied by political revolution, but the modern world was initiated by another kind of revolution; that of industry. The development of steam power at the end of the eighteenth century changed what had been a predominantly rural population to an urban one and the cities at the heart of industry grew rapidly.

IRON AND STEEL

The new materials of the industrial revolution, such as wrought iron and steel, were quickly transferred into construction applications. This development marked a paradigm shift from bespoke, heavy, load-bearing construction to lightweight factory-produced building elements. The world celebrated the new products of mass production through a series of trade exhibitions. Most architecturally notable were those in London in 1851 and Paris in 1855. In London, the exhibition was housed in the enormous custom-built structure of Crystal Palace.

Designed by **Joseph Paxton**, the Crystal Palace used standard components of prefabricated cast iron lattice which was infilled with glass panels to form a greenhouse of enormous proportions. Paxton's Crystal Palace used these newly available materials to their limit, borrowing traditional forms and structurally reinterpreting them.

In Paris, the properties of cast iron showed how lightweight construction could be employed to achieve previously unseen heights. The Eiffel Tower soared some 312 metres in the Parisian skyline and its skeleton frame was to be the forerunner of the tall buildings and skyscrapers that were to follow.

But the opportunity to show what could really be achieved fell to the US. In 1871 a fire destroyed much of the city of Chicago. Faced with a blank sheet for the city, architects again used the framing principle as a basis for construction but this time with steel, far stronger and proportionately lighter than iron. It was used to construct the first high-rise building in the world.

Louis Sullivan, credited with the phrase 'form follows function', was perhaps the first great architect of the modern age. His Carson Pirie Scott building (in Chicago), was a simple frame structure that allowed clear expression without decoration. This was a radical break from the classical ornamentation that had previously characterised much civic building.

Joseph Paxton 1803–1865

Paxton was an English architect and keen gardener. His work at Chatsworth House in Derbyshire saw him experiment with framed glass structures that would allow him to grow and protect sensitive and delicate plants. From these Paxton developed designs to build the Crystal Palace for London's Great Exhibition in 1851.

The project was the most innovative use of glass and steel at the time and was of an unprecedented scale. The Crystal Palace was intended to be a temporary structure, but was moved to Sydenham in South London after the exhibition had finished.

16. The Iron Bridge at Coalbrookdale, UK
T M Pritchard, 1777–1779

The world's first cast-iron bridge was built over the River Severn at Coalbrookdale, England, by Abraham Darby III, and is now recognised as one of the great symbols of the Industrial Revolution. The bridge had a far-reaching impact on local society and the economy, on bridge design and on the use of cast iron in building. It represents the new technology and engineering potential of the eighteenth century. The bridge translates the previous idea of a heavy stone structure into a light, elegant, almost transparent frame.

16

17. The Penguin Pool at London Zoo, London, UK
Lubetkin Drake & Tecton, 1934
This pool design uses a ramp constructed from reinforced concrete, which creates a striking sculptural element linking two levels. It exploits the potential of concrete, demonstrating both structural and dynamic qualities.

18. The Barcelona Pavilion (interior), constructed for the International Exposition in Barcelona of 1929
Ludwig Mies van der Rohe, 1928–1929
The Barcelona Pavilion was the German Pavilion for the 1929 World's Fair in Barcelona. It was an important building in the history of modern architecture, known for its simple form and use of extravagant materials, such as marble and travertine.

19. The Barcelona Pavilion (exterior), constructed for the International Exposition in Barcelona of 1929
Ludwig Mies van der Rohe, 1928–1929
The pavilion's structure consisted of eight steel posts supporting a flat roof, with curtain glass walling and a handful of partition walls. The overall impression is of perpendicular planes in three dimensions forming a cool, luxurious space. The pavilion was demolished at the end of the exhibition, but a copy has since been built on the same site.

17

18

19

GLASS AND CONCRETE

Along with iron and steel, two other materials also came to characterise the modern movement: sheet glass and reinforced concrete. Mies van der Rohe had seen the possibilities of new float glass production methods, which could create a material that would enable transparency and structural honesty, and would herald a spirit of openness that was to mark the new utopian age of the twentieth century. Mies van der Rohe's Barcelona Pavilion design, an exposition building constructed in Catalonia in 1929, reduced the structure to a series of columns that supported a flat roof, with non-loadbearing partition walls made of glass and thin veneers of fine marble to divide the spaces within. In conceiving architecture as a spatial continuity from inside to outside, Mies van der Rohe also broke the historic paradigm of the interior being a series of spaces enclosed by solid load-bearing walls and punctured by windows and doors. Instead, he produced an open plan in which space flowed seamlessly through the building, unhindered by the mass and solidity of the structure. His was the 'new' architecture: open, light and elegant.

Ludwig Mies van der Rohe 1886–1969

Born in Germany, Mies van der Rohe was part of the group that established the Bauhaus school (see page 132). He was an architect, teacher, furniture designer and urban planner, who questioned all aspects of design. Mies van der Rohe also questioned the idea of walls, floors and ceilings, reinventing architectural language to become planes and points.

Mies van der Rohe's significant buildings include the Barcelona Pavilion and the Seagram Building in New York. These buildings are two of the most important pieces of twentieth-century architecture in terms of their use of material and subsequent form.

20. Le Modulor

Le Corbusier, 1943–1947
Le Corbusier explicitly used the golden ratio (see page 117) in his modular system for the scale of architectural proportion. He saw this system as a continuation of the long tradition of Vitruvius, Leonardo da Vinci's Vitruvian Man, the work of Leon Battista Alberti, and others who used the proportions of the human body to improve the appearance and function of architecture. In addition to the golden ratio, Le Corbusier based his system on human measurements, Fibonacci numbers, and the double unit. He took da Vinci's suggestion of the golden ratio in human proportions to an extreme: he sectioned his model human body's height at the navel with the two sections in golden ratio, then subdivided those sections in golden ratio at the knees and throat; he used these golden ratio proportions in the modular system.

20

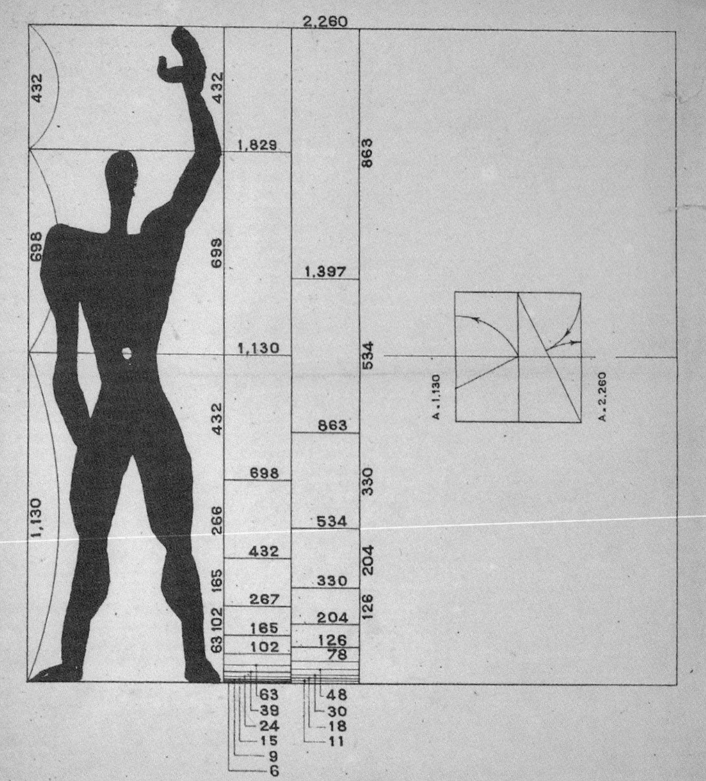

PURISM

During the modernist period Swiss architect Le Corbusier (born Charles Jeanneret) established principles of architecture that responded to Renaissance ideas and dogma. These governing rules were less about determining the form and more about establishing a direction for an architectural response.

Another important development for Le Corbusier was the modular system that, following the tradition of Leonardo da Vinci and Leon Battista Alberti amongst others, suggested that architecture needs to be centred around the proportion of the human body. The concept of le modulor created a measuring system that used human anthropometric dimensions as a way of determining form and space, and this system informed and underpinned the design of Le Corbusier's furniture, buildings and spaces.

Characteristics of Modernist Architecture

1. Pilotis: these are columns elevating the mass of the building off the ground.
2. The Free Plan: this is achieved through the separation of the load-bearing columns from the walls subdividing the space.
3. The free façade: this is the result of the free plan in the vertical plane.
4. The long, horizontal ribbon window.
5. The roof garden: this restores the area of ground covered by the structure.

21. The Schröder House, Utrecht, The Netherlands
Gerrit Rietveld, 1924–1925
The Schröder house is a kind of three-dimensional puzzle; it takes space and connects it both vertically and horizontally, using colour to signify the vertical and horizontal planes. The interior walls move to reveal larger open spaces. Everything is reinvented inside the house, all processes of living have been observed and responded to. The bathroom needs to be discovered and is unveiled in a cupboard. Sleeping, sitting and living are interweaved in one space. It is an experiment of space, form and function.

21

DE STIJL

In the twentieth century the Dutch artistic movement, De Stijl (the style) began to connect the ideas of artists such as **Theo van Doesburg** to the notion of physical space. In the *De Stijl* journal van Doesburg explored the notion of space in relation to surface and colour. Similarly Gerrit Rietveld developed ideas of space, form and colour in the design of his furniture and architecture.

Proponents of De Stijl sought to express a new utopian ideal of spiritual harmony and order. They advocated pure abstraction and universality by a reduction to the essentials of form and colour. They simplified visual compositions to the vertical and horizontal directions, and used only primary colours along with black and white.

Theo van Doesburg 1883–1931
Theo van Doesburg was one the founders of the De Stijl (the style) movement, which was concerned primarily with ideas of art and architecture. Interested in abstraction of colour and form, De Stijl employed a visual code that connected colour and plane. Primary colours and black and white were used in both art and architecture to explore space and form.

Chapter 3
Construction

Construction is about the making of architecture; its physicality and its materiality. A building can be considered at a macro level, as a structural frame with a roof, walls and floors, but it simultaneously needs to be considered as a series of details that explain how the architectural components are combined and unified. For example, a building must operate and function effectively with design systems such as ventilation, heating or lighting, which provide variable and comfortable internal environments. Essentially, a building is a kind of machine; a series of interdependent parts and systems that collectively enable it to be effective and habitable.

1. 2•4•6•8 House Assembly Drawing
Morphosis Architects, 1978
This is an exploded isonometric drawing that shows every component part of a house in California, from the inner structure right through to the window frames. The drawing reveals how each component connects together to create an assembled single piece.

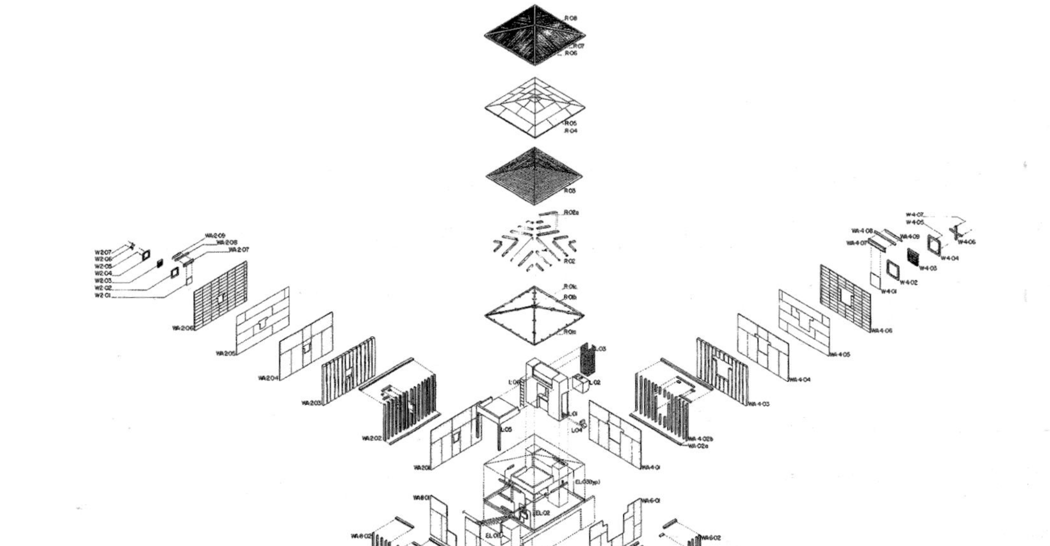

1

2·4·6·8 HOUSE© MOD. # MOR-746·747

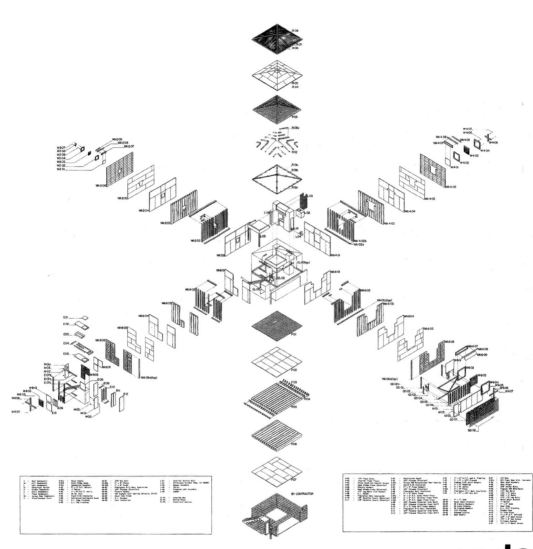

Materials

Construction techniques and systems are many and varied, but each is informed by the materials that are used.

This section will serve as an introduction to the typical materials used in construction, and will demonstrate how each can be used to provide a texture, form and spatial definition to a building.

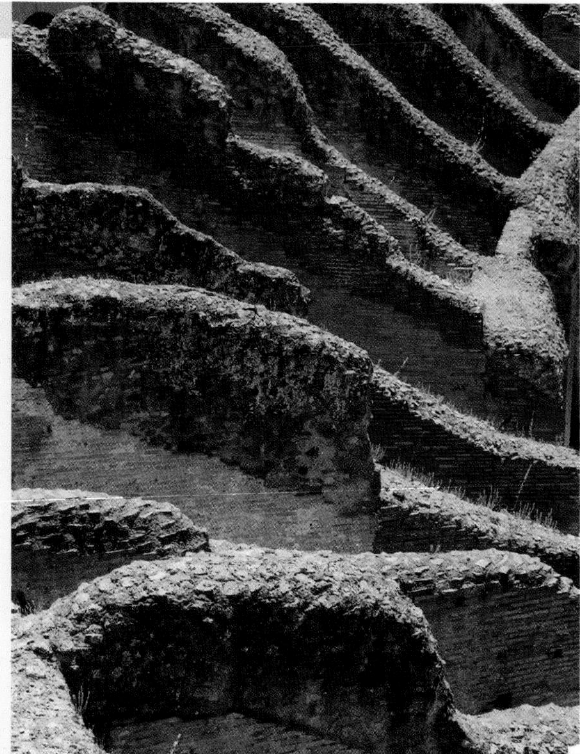

MASONRY

Masonry is typified by constructions made from materials of the earth, such as brick and stone. When used in construction, masonry is a material that is stacked; traditionally heavier elements are placed on the lower layers and lighter layers are used as one moves vertically from the foundations to the roof. Some masonry construction is modular and as such it needs to behave in a particular way. For example, when openings are created in a brick wall, it is necessary to support the brickwork above. Typically voussoirs (a wedge-shaped or tapered brick or stone) are used to produce arches in a masonry wall, which provides the required support. Understanding the properties of masonry is an important part of understanding architecture that uses it. For example, bricks need to be stacked alternately, because if the courses are not varied the wall will be unstable and collapse.

The effect of a brick wall will vary according to the coursing patterns and brick colours available. Practically, a brick wall needs additional support over a certain height or it will not be stable, also it needs substantial support in its foundation to provide stability. Such concerns will ultimately inform the architectural design.

2. Colosseum (detail), Rome, Italy
AD c.70–82
The Colosseum in Rome is made from many materials including brick. As time has passed the masonry has eroded to create a dynamic sculpted effect on the surface.

3. Brick House, London, UK
Caruso St John, 2005
The floors and walls of this house are built of brick, inside and out. The use of one material binds the whole building. The arrangement of bricks within the mortar shifts as surfaces stretch, bend and twist, making them appear elastic and dynamic.

CONCRETE

Concrete is made of aggregate, gravel, cement, sand and water. It is the variable proportional quantities of these materials that give concrete its intrinsic strength.

Concrete can be brutal when used in large, heavy structures, but it can also have a subtlety to it, a quality that is exploited by Japanese architect **Tadao Ando**. In his architecture the shuttering, which supports the concrete while it is setting, is used to provide texture to the finished building. The memory of the shuttering's timber grain and the fixing bolts for the concrete's mould or formwork remain on the wall finish, giving the walls a depth and a sense of surface.

Sometimes concrete is reinforced with a steel mesh to provide greater strength and stability. Reinforced concrete can span large distances and is used in engineering projects such as road building and bridge construction. Reinforced concrete allows enormous flexibility with large-scale structures.

The use of reinforced concrete was pioneered by French architect Auguste Perret. At the beginning of the twentieth century, Perret first worked alongside Le Corbusier and Peter Behrens, the German exponent of 'industrial design'. Behrens admired the engineer's ethic of mass production, logical design and function over style. Le Corbusier brought together the material and stylistic influences of Perret and Behrens in his 'Maison Dom-ino' plan of 1915 (see pages 72–73). This house would be made of reinforced concrete and was intended for mass production, but was also flexible: none of the walls were load-bearing and so the interior could be arranged as the occupant wished. Le Corbusier's radical ideas were given expression in his 1923 book *Vers Une Architecture* ('Towards a New Architecture'). 'A house', Le Corbusier intoned from its pages, 'is a machine for living in'.

Tadao Ando b. 1941

Ando is heavily influenced by the Japanese sense of materiality in construction. Light and space are important aspects of his work. Ando is most famously renowned for his use of concrete and application of simple geometry to plan, section and elevation.

Ando favours the use of timber shuttering, which he uses to create the 'mould' or formwork for in situ concrete (concrete poured on site). When the shuttering is removed the pattern of the timber and the bolts that connected it are still left on the concrete. This surface effect is a distinctive aspect of his work.

4. The Collection: Art and Archaeology, Lincolnshire, UK
Panter Hudspith Architects, 2005
This museum uses materials sensitively. The high quality timber finish creates a soft feel to the interior with light entering from above, highlighting the concrete wall. The light across the surface reveals the marks of the shuttering used to hold the concrete as it is set, giving it texture and definition.

5. Kidosaki House, Tokyo, Japan
Tadao Ando, 1982–1986
This house displays Ando's signature technique of building with concrete and the incorporation of the aesthetic produced from using timber shuttering. The holes in the walls indicate the position of the bolts that were used to hold together the shuttering.

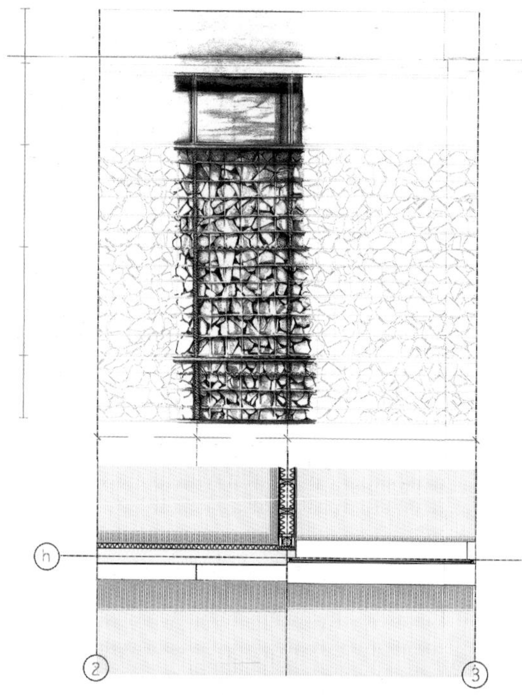

GABION AND DRY-STONE WALLS

Gabion walls are retaining walls that are used to hold back earthworks or in the remodelling of landscapes for road construction or sea defences. A gabion wall is essentially a steel cage filled with large grade stones. They are very easy to construct on difficult sites, and produce a quick-to-assemble and natural wall. Gabion walls have often been used as a form of architectural cladding to give a particular aesthetic to a building.

Dry-stone walls are constructed from found materials. Traditionally used to define boundaries, they are a precursor to gabion walls. Dry-stone walls require little skill to build and as the materials used to construct them are found on-site, there are no transportation methods to consider. These walls can be easily maintained too.

6. Gabion Wall
Gabion walls are a metal framework or cage filled with stones of varying sizes. This example is a retaining wall at the edge of a road.

7. Pencil Sketch of a Gabion Wall
This drawing uses pencil to give a sense of depth to the stones used in gabion construction, each stone can be clearly identified and defined from the cage that contains them.

8. Downland Gridshell Weald and Downland Museum, West Sussex, UK
Edward Cullinan Architects, 1996–2002
This is an example of a grid shell timber frame. The main structure is made of oak laths (strips of timber) connected in a grid pattern that was then gradually lowered and bent into place. This has then been covered in timber tiles.

9. Traditional Japanese Timber Frame House
This traditional Japanese house uses timber as the structural frame of the building. The timber frame raises the structure off the ground. The roof structure overhangs the main building, protecting it from sunlight and rain. In this example, the architect's choice of materials has responded directly to the local site conditions.

Timber can be used both as an exterior frame or an interior finish. Some building types use timber for the structure or frame, the floor finish and the wall finish inside and out. Buildings constructed of timber were originally part of local traditions. A log cabin was built from the trees of the surrounding forest, it needed little transportation and assembly on site was quick.

Tradesmen who work with timber are carpenters if they deal with larger structural pieces of timber, or joiners if they make the finished elements for the interior such as stairs or doors. The more detailed furnishing elements are made by cabinetmakers.

Timber framed buildings are usually of a limited scale; their limitation is caused by the size of the available material. Timber is cut to standard sizes and these work with other prefabricated components of the construction industry (such as doors and windows), and allow easy transportation and handling on-site.

Timber comes in various forms, it can be rough and textured or planed and finished, the choice will depend on where and how it is to be used. Timber is ultimately a flexible and natural material; it is light and easily adaptable on site and its natural colour and texture provide a range of finishes. When using timber, an important consideration for the architect is to ensure that the wood is sustainably sourced and harvested responsibly.

Vladimir Tatlin 1885–1953

Tatlin became one of the two most important figures in the Russian avant-garde art movement of the 1920s. Tatlin achieved fame as the architect who designed the huge Monument to the Third International, also known as Tatlin's Tower. Planned in 1920, the monument was to be a tall tower made from iron, glass and steel, which would have dwarfed the Eiffel Tower in Paris (it was a third taller at 396 metres high). Inside the iron-and-steel structure of twin spirals, the design envisaged three building blocks, covered with glass windows, which would rotate at different speeds (the first one, a cube, once a year; the second one, a pyramid, once a month; the third one, a cylinder, once a day).

IRON AND STEEL

Iron and steel (an iron alloy mixed with carbon and other elements) can be used to construct the light frames that support a building, or to clad a building, providing a metal finish that can be both distinctive and durable.

Iron-frame buildings became popular during the period of nineteenth-century industrialisation and structures such as London's Crystal Palace and the Eiffel Tower in Paris challenged the scale of structural possibility. Futuristic concepts such as **Vladimir Tatlin's** tower imagined an ambitious structure that would see the halls of state moving within a metal framework.

The concepts and constructions of the nineteenth century inspired many steel-framed buildings in the US and in Asia, which scaled previously unimagined heights. Important examples are the Chrysler Building in New York and the tallest building of the twentieth century, the Petronas Towers in Kuala Lumpur.

Steel has liberated architectural form and has afforded the potential for a skyscraper scale of architecture. It is the ultimate flexible, durable and strong material. It can be manufactured off-site and individual elements can be bolted together. Materials such as these take architectural engineering expertise to its limits and enables the creation of impressive structures that can withstand the forces of nature.

10

10. The Eiffel Tower, Paris, France
Gustave Eiffel, 1887–1889
Designed as a temporary structure to celebrate the potential of engineering in France, the Eiffel Tower is made from iron using a limited number of prefabricated parts.

11. The Greater London Authority Building (interior), London, UK
Foster + Partners, 2002
The GLA building or (city hall) is located on the banks of the River Thames, and is the headquarters of the London Assembly and the city's council. The architect's use of glass in this building is significant, it both reflects the transparent nature of democracy and is part of the building's sustainable strategy (as the glazed outer wall allows light into the building and passively heats the building in winter). The outer wall also frames incredible views from within the building across the River Thames.

GLASS

Glass is an exciting material because it has so many possibilities. It can appear as an invisible plane (as it is transparent), but it can also manipulate and filter light to create areas of shadow and light inside a building. Innovation in technology means that glass can now be used structurally in certain applications to challenge our sense of space and surface.

The origins of glass are Phoenician and Egyptian (circa 2500 BC when it was used to produce decorative ceramics and jewellery) and the material is made by fusing the most basic natural materials: sand, soda and lime. Glass has been used as a construction material since the eleventh century, when techniques were developed that enabled glass to be manufactured in sheets.

The use of glass has transformed the way buildings have been designed. It allows a definition between the inside and outside of a building, and defines a space with light. It has evolved to become a high-technology product.

Nowadays for example, glass can self-clean if coated with titanium oxide, which absorbs ultra-violet rays and, through a chemical process, gradually and continuously breaks down any organic mater that builds up on the surface, which is then washed away by rainwater. Laminated glass can incorporate layers of coloured glass, which react to changes in temperature and so alter the mood inside a space. Similarly, 'smart' glass can vary the amount of heat and light passing through it using electro-chromic and liquid crystal technologies. Privalite glass allows an electrical current to turn transparent glass into an opaque screen by realigning electrons within the construction of the glass sheet, and Pilkington K glass separates the different types of radiation passing through it to prevent buildings from overheating.

Glass possesses the unique quality of allowing interior spaces to appear as though they are actually part of the outside, of nature, or part of a greater whole.

Elements of Construction

At its most basic level, there are four major elements in any building's construction: the structure (or framework), the foundations, the roof and the walls and openings. Once these elements are determined the building will have a defined form, and only then can the more detailed design decisions be considered.

STRUCTURE

In this context, structure is concerned with how the building is supported, and this usually takes one of two forms: structures of solid construction (where the walls support the building) or structures of framework construction (where the frame is independent of the building's walls and floors).

As the name suggests solid construction creates a heaviness and solidity to buildings and will define a building's interior spaces. It creates a permanent and massive sense of the architectural form. Solid construction can use masonry, which can be modules of natural stone or brick, or it may be achieved using concrete, either prefabricated (made off-site) or in situ (poured into moulds on-site).

Using a frame construction provides a great deal of flexibility in terms of the building's internal layout and the position of its openings (such as doors and windows). The structural frame can be made of many materials such as timber, steel or concrete, and it can be very quickly constructed and even adapted to suit future needs.

A classic example of a framework construction is Le Corbusier's conceptual Dom-ino frame. It is a concrete frame that connects the floor planes and the roof plane with a single staircase. Doing so allows the internal and external walls to be positioned so as to respond to the internal arrangement of the building. This structure led to the birth of the 'free' plan.

The free plan was a revolutionary concept because it proposed that the walls and openings were not dependent on a building's structure. Instead, a framework gave freedom to the internal layout of the plan and the position of its doors and windows. This concept is exemplified by Le Corbusier's Villa Savoye in Poitiers, north of Paris.

12

12. Musée du Quai Branly, Paris, France
Jean Nouvel, 2006
This museum is located alongside the River Seine in Paris, France. The museum is surrounded by a glazed screen that separates the garden space acoustically from the busy road, but maintains the visual connection to the Seine. The screen also enhances the idea that the garden serves as an introduction to the museum. It is also an independent structure that defines the museum's garden.

13. The Dom-ino Frame
The title of Le Corbusier's theoretical study of a structural frame originates from the Latin for house: 'domus'. The Dom-ino frame was conceived as an affordable prefabricated system that would free interior and exterior walls from structural restraints.

13

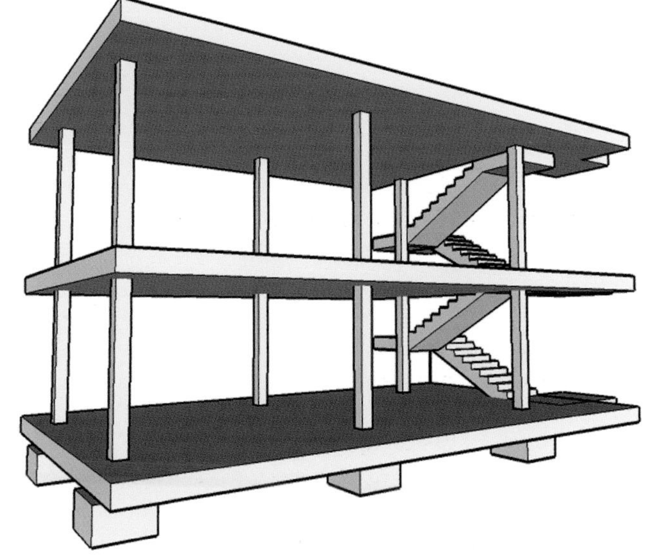

14. Diagram of the Pyramide du Louvre's Foundations
This diagram shows that the glazed structure of the Pyramide du Louvre is actually the tip of the building, which extends beneath the ground.

15. Pyramide du Louvre, Paris, France
I. M. Pei, 1989
The Pyramide du Louvre was a later addition to the original museum. The structure above ground is an entrance portico to the museum's main galleries and an introduction to the subterranean spaces beneath. The glazed structure brings light into the museum spaces beneath ground.

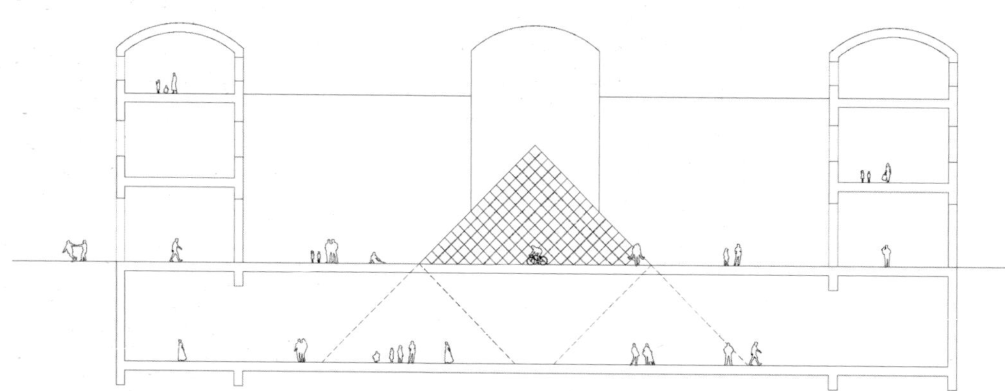
14

FOUNDATION

The structure of the building has to be supported at the point where it touches the ground; this support is usually referred to as the building's foundation. The foundation essentially supports the frame or walls of the structure and needs to be sufficiently strong to respond to the ground conditions around the building and any anticipated movement. Ground movement will be affected by local conditions such as the geology of the site, in particular, the dryness of the ground. Large structures or trees nearby could also affect the stability of the building. A structural engineer would normally advise on the type of foundations that would best respond to the building design and the site ground conditions.

15

There are many buildings, for reasons of local topography, required functionality or restrictions of site development, which are built partially or wholly underground. In urban centres where there is often pressure on land values, this can be a financially viable proposition.

In some climates building underground can provide an extra dimension of protection from the environment. These types of subterranean building require specific construction methods; essentially a retaining wall (a wall that is holding back the soil or earth) is required to define the building's structure, and this needs to be both insulated and made to incorporate a waterproof layer to prevent water penetration from the surrounding ground.

16

17

WALLS AND OPENINGS

The wall is an architectural aspect that creates an enclosure, marking the definition between the interior and exterior boundaries. Walls can be load bearing, supporting a roof or floor plane, or be non-load bearing, acting simply as a division of space.

Curtain walls are an example of external walls that are non-load bearing, and are used to define inside space from outside space. They are waterproof and designed to cope with external dynamic pressures. Originally, curtain walls were made from steel, but are now more commonly made from a light metal frame that is infilled with glass, metals or veneers such as timber or stone.

Openings in walls allow light into the interior spaces, provide ventilation and also, critically, allow entry to and exit from a building or space. Any opening compromises the idea of enclosure and separates the internal climate from the external climate. For this reason, openings need to be considered very carefully and in great detail.

The door opening is often the most celebrated aspect of any elevation as it marks the point of entry and often defines a building's identity. Doorways are often marked by thresholds, which are raised steps or plinths that serve to further define the point of entry. Canopies or covering structures can also provide a sense of shelter at a doorway.

Windows tend to vary in size to reflect the range of activities that are likely to take place inside, and the kind of light, view and privacy expected by the building's occupants. Picture windows frame views across rural or urban landscapes to reduce the sense of separation between the inside and the outside.

16. Glazed Curtain Wall, Bull Ring Shopping Centre, Birmingham, UK
Glass can act as a wall. Although not a visual barrier, it can create definition between a building's inside and outside. In this curtain wall the glazing is hung off a steel frame inside.

17. Exterior Folding Blind
Blinds can be placed on the inside or outside of a window to modify the light coming inside. If they can fold or move they provide a very adaptable system, allowing the building to respond to changing light throughout the day.

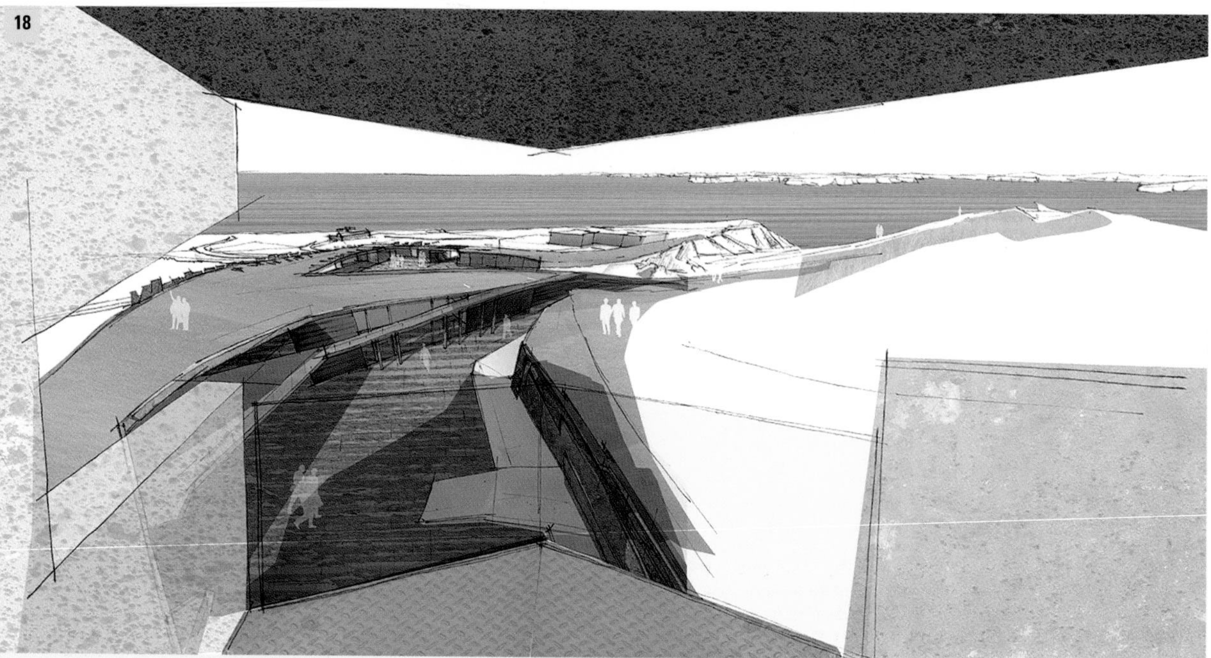

ROOFS

The roof defines the top layer of a building; it offers protection and provides a sense of safety and security. A roof can be extensive, acting as a structure that is independent of the building or buildings that it covers, or it can be precisely related to the building outline it covers.

The roof of a building is normally determined by its function, but the building's immediate context will also inform the roof's design. For example, if there are pitched roofs in the vicinity then this will probably create a precedent for a particular formal response.

Climate is also a determining factor. Rainfall needs to be quickly and efficiently drained away, which might dictate the necessity of a sloped roof. In very warm climates, a roof offers protection from the intense heat and overhanging roof structures can provide additional shelter to the streets below. In climates where snow is a consideration, the roof pitch is critical to prevent snow settling on the roof surface.

18. Giants' Causeway Competition Proposal
David Mathias and Peter Williams, 2005
The roof can form a significant part of the architectural concept. This competition proposal for a visitor centre in Northern Ireland integrates the roof as a part of the surrounding landscape. The roof forms part of an extended journey that connects to the building idea.

19. Villa Savoye Roof Garden, Paris, France
Le Corbusier, 1928–1929
The roof of a building can provide an area of additional inhabitable space. Le Corbusier's machine for living, Villa Savoye, has a series of connected roof gardens providing additional exterior space.

19

Prefabrication

Prefabricated constructions describe those buildings whose parts or components have been specifically manufactured to enable easy assembly on site. Prefabricated components can range from a small factory-made element such as a chair, to larger construction elements such as pre-cast concrete slabs, and even whole housing units that are installed and assembled on-site. Prefabricated elements can be partially assembled off-site and then finished on-site, or be supplied fully finished and ready to use.

Richard Rogers's Lloyds Building in London (constructed 1979–1984) used prefabricated toilet units, which were hoisted into place and bolted onto the structure. This revelation saved enormous amounts of construction time and allowed units to be made in factory-controlled conditions, precisely and efficiently.

Prefabrication techniques have developed enormously since then. Huf Haus is a German company, one of many that provides buildings almost in kit form, as a series of prefabricated elements that arrive on-site and are bolted together to produce a perfect factory-machined result. Whole blocks of housing have been produced in this way; units are first fitted out and then transported to site and slotted into preformed structures.

Prefabrication brings many advantages including speed of construction and assembly, strict quality control (all elements are made in factories where there are fewer variables than on a building site) and the production of adaptable, light and mobile structures that have a flexible quality as they could be dismantled and erected elsewhere.

20

21

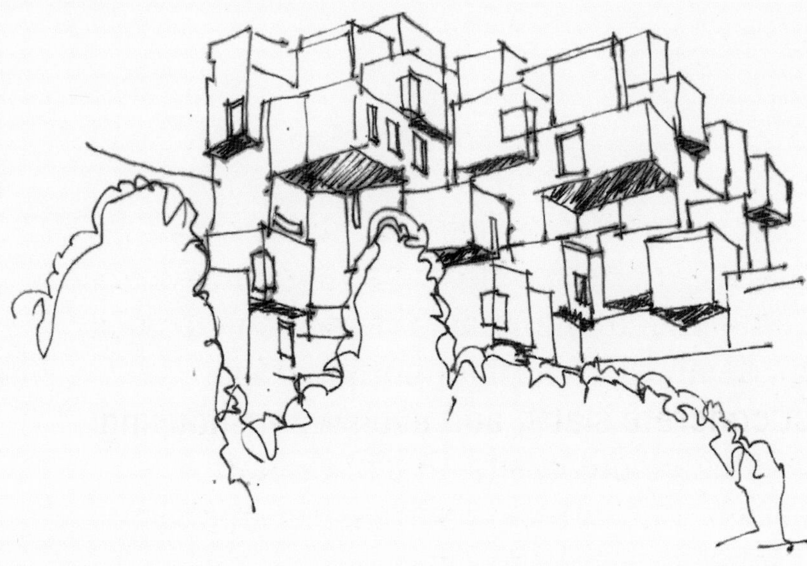

20. London Prefabricated Housing Scheme
Individual prefabricated elements such as bathroom units can be dropped into place during construction. These elements could be as big as a whole housing unit. The limitations are transportation and installation factors.

21. Prefabricated Habitat Housing Student Sketch
This experimental housing block was built in 1967 for the World's Fair in Montreal. It demonstrates the concept of stacking prefabricated units to create an apartment block or settlement.

22. Prefabricated Architecture Student Scheme
This image indicates how a housing scheme could be developed with different prefabricated elements, each one dropped in at a different stage of the project's lifespan.

22

Reinvention

Our cities offer numerous possibilities to reinvent structures or forms that are part of the identity of its skyline or architectural heritage, and which have been made redundant through changing uses of spaces and places. Reinvention is an opportunity that architects can respond to positively. Doing so requires sensitive and careful consideration of the history of the site, in particular how an existing building can adapt to new functions without compromising important aspects of its character and form.

Reinventing existing buildings through design is often a more sustainable way to deal with the structure, as it will incorporate existing forms and materials.

A good example of this is the Tate Modern gallery in London. Now an extremely successful gallery, the building was a redundant power station that was reinvented by Swiss architects Herzog and de Meuron in 2000. The Tate Modern has since become one of the most famous art galleries in the world. The design used the impact and scale of the existing building to great effect. It acts as a beacon, responding to the building's site on the south bank of the River Thames in London. Other elements such as a bridge and a riverside walk created the urban infrastructure that makes the gallery now a central part of its surrounding location.

23. The Great Court at the British Museum, London, UK
Foster + Partners, 1994–2000
The Great Court was originally an underused external courtyard that was reinvented by Foster + Partners in 1994. The area was covered with a unique glazed structure to become a vibrant internal courtyard serving as café, reception and information spaces for the museum.

24. The Tate Modern, London, UK
Herzog and de Meuron 1998–2000
The construction of the Tate Modern formed part of a redevelopment of London's South Bank. This former power station was redefined; its external form was already powerful and iconic – the internal spaces such as the turbine hall were industrial in scale – and this was used to dramatic effect in the gallery's central exhibition space, allowing large-scale exhibits and events to be staged.

23

Foster + Partners

Norman Foster's practice is concerned with 'hi-tech' architecture that uses modern technology and intelligent materials. Foster + Partners has been involved in projects ranging from product and building design to refurbishment and urban master planning. Innovative use of glass has always been a feature of its work.

Recent projects include the Great Court at the British Museum, the Hong Kong and Shanghai Bank, the Reichstag redesign and the international airport terminal in Beijing.

24

25. BedZED Eco-community Development, Surrey, UK
Bill Dunster Architects, 2002
Beddington Zero Energy Development (BedZED) is the UK's largest zero energy development. It has housing and work spaces that are designed specifically as an approach to sustainable living in the city. The development uses energy from renewable resources and includes solar energy systems and waste-water recycling.

Sustainability

Designing buildings raises many issues concerning sustainability. At a macro level, the design of a city for example, there are issues of transportation, energy efficiency or carbon emissions to resolve; at the micro level the design of individual buildings, the types of materials used and how they are manufactured and sourced are important considerations in sustainable architectural design.

Sustainability is a very broad term when applied to architecture and refers to the nature of the construction, the materials used and their origins. For example, does a timber specified for a particular project come from a sustainable resource? Is it from a managed forest where each tree removed is replaced by another tree, or is it from a hardwood forest, where the removal of trees is causing irreparable damage to the area and ultimately the planet?

There are broader issues to consider in the context of sustainability. For example, how far do the materials that are used in a building travel to get to the site? If slate from China is used in a building in Europe, the financial cost may be less than locally sourced materials, but the carbon cost in terms of fuel used to transport these materials is significant. The carbon footprint of a building is the amount of carbon expended to make the materials and transport those materials to the site. Whenever materials are sourced or specified these considerations should be taken into account.

Another consideration is the energy efficiency of the building over its lifetime. Insulation, for example, is essential to reduce the amount of fuel needed to maintain the building at a comfortable ambient temperature. Is the energy used to power the building renewable? How are waste products treated and disposed of? All such questions of sustainability need to be considered as the building design develops.

25

Innovative Materials

Advances in material technologies present new opportunities for contemporary architecture. Material innovations from arenas such as fashion and product design can also inform building design. These innovations may be concerned with the application of technologies to make living easier or the use of products to make living more sustainable or exciting.

Interactive technologies provide the potential for buildings to respond to user activities. Movement sensors in and around buildings allow services such as lighting and ventilation to operate remotely. Materials can also react to movement or light through thermal sensors, and wireless technologies allow much greater flexibility in the way we use buildings.

Combining materials can increase a material's flexibility and application opportunities. Composite glass flooring for example, which is made from structural glass and aluminium, combines the lightness and strength of aluminium with the transparency of glass to create large glass panels that can also be used as floor panels because they are weight bearing.

Translucent or transparent concrete, which is made from glass and polymerised synthetics, has revolutionised the properties of concrete. As well as great flexibility (as it can be poured and moulded), it has the added benefit of allowing light to pass through it. Structural columns using this material become visibly lighter as a result.

The increased demand for energy efficiency in buildings, and the potential to make surfaces a source of harnessing energy, has meant that the solar panel has become more prevalent and more flexible in its application. Solar panels can now be an integrated part of a roof system, rather than treated as a bolt-on element, and this presents the architect with increased design opportunities.

Innovation can also mean using materials in a new context. Reflective materials, traditionally used in aerospace design, are now being used in roofing insulation. Sheep's wool is often used in building insulation as it has a high thermal value. Straw bales, once a localised building material, are now viewed as a sustainable material for many different contexts.

The future of construction materials and technology is interwoven with the development of 'smart' materials from a variety of industries. Ascertaining how these technologies and innovations can be incorporated into building materials and strategies, to make living and working a more dynamic and interactive experience, is the challenge facing architects today.

26

26. Straw Bale Structure, Epping Green, Hertfordshire, UK
Yasmin Shariff, Denis Sharp Architects, 1999
Some 120 straw bales were used to construct this building's wall, and each has been gently worked into a small drum-like structure. The architect wanted to echo the idea of a mud hut, as this would in turn reflect the use of the building (for cultural dance and music classes). Tucked away in a small wooded area, the straw bales and the salvaged wood used to build the dance studio provide it with a sense of belonging, while not intruding on the natural landscape.

27. The Selfridges Store at the Bullring, Birmingham, UK
Future Systems, 1993–2003
This building is organic in form, and is covered in some 15,000 aluminium discs that further exaggerate and dramatise the exterior of the building. The store's dynamic shape demands an innovative covering or cladding that reflects the architectural concept.

27

Chapter 4
Representation

In this context, representation refers to the range of methods that can be used to communicate architectural ideas and concepts. Some of these techniques are traditionally associated with architectural expression (such as plan, section, and elevation drawings), and others are borrowed or adapted from other disciplines, such as storyboarding from film production, computer-generated imagery from areas of digital media, or freehand sketching and analytical drawing techniques that are most commonly associated with fine art.

1. CAD Scheme
This is a computer-generated image that shows a proposed scheme for a site in Venice, Italy. The use of colour and shadow gives depth and texture to this section drawing. The placement of figures in the drawing provides a sense of scale and proportion.

1

CAD Drawing

Over the last 20 years technological advances have presented a range of new possibilities for architects. All students now learn some form of Computer Aided Design (CAD) skills at schools of architecture and it is now an accepted language in the discourse of the discipline.

This technological advance has presented a whole new interface to describe architectural spaces and has allowed new sorts of architectural forms to evolve.

FACILITATING OR LIMITING?

At one level, CAD provides an exploratory design tool; different software packages, used independently or collectively, allow for new initiatives and forms of expression. CAD also allows for quick translation of ideas because plan and section drawings can be easily adapted and developed. CAD can also be used to produce a series of related images, each one providing an additional layer of information. Collectively the series will form a 'package' of information that will better communicate the concept or construction instructions.

Sometimes, however, the computer can be seen as a limiting factor. The CAD image renders as a graphic, which can be seductive and impressive, but it's still the architecture as built, inhabitable space, that needs to be tested and read as a believable three-dimensional form.

There are interesting interfaces in the use of CAD; some of the expressions of the buildings can appear surreal, while other interpretations can sometimes appear so real and so perfect in their imagery, that one is forced to ask whether the representation is a photograph of reality or a computer-generated model.

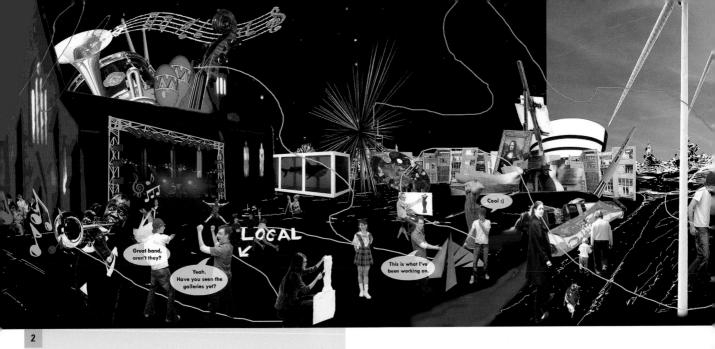

2

PHOTOMONTAGE

A very effective mechanism in CAD drawing is the photomontage technique. It produces a seductive image that is often used as a means to convince or demonstrate that the architecture can 'fit' any proposed client requirements or is appropriate for its intended site. Photomontage images are frequently described as artist impressions because they often mix digital photographs of an existing site with computer-generated models. Photomontage images are essentially 'stage managed' by the designer to obtain the best view or the most impressive angle of the proposed idea The underlying aim of any representation technique will be to display the concept at its best.

3

2. New Urban Space
European Studio Photomontage, 2006
Using CAD drawings and photographs of real places and people can produce an image that brings together a range of eclectic representational techniques. This allows an understanding of how a place or idea might appear in reality.

3. CAD Photomontage
Here a CAD model is superimposed over a series of site photographs to suggest the scale of the proposed building on the site.

4

4., 5. & 6. Sketchbook Pages
These pages from a variety of sketchbooks show a range of quickly drawn concepts that explore different design ideas and possibilities. These sketches range from quick thoughts (4), to considered concepts (5), and the exploration of an idea within an existing reality (6).

Sketching

Architectural drawing tends to fall into one of three broad categories: conceptual, developmental and realisation. The sketch drawing can exist across all categories, however it is used most readily at the conceptual stage because it is the quickest and simplest way to explain complex ideas in architecture.

Sketches can be quick and inspired or more detailed and produced to scale. There are even software packages available that attempt to recreate the loose dynamic aspect of sketching (such as Google SketchUp). There is power in a sketch; it is a personal and immediate connection between the idea and the rendering of a two-dimensional representation on paper. A sketch has character and it lacks precision, which is its attraction. In the sleight of the hand, the thickness of the pencil line, all sorts of issues can be implied and hidden. Sketching happens at all stages of the design process, but in particular at the start of it, when the detail hasn't yet been considered, allowing the potential for anything to happen.

5

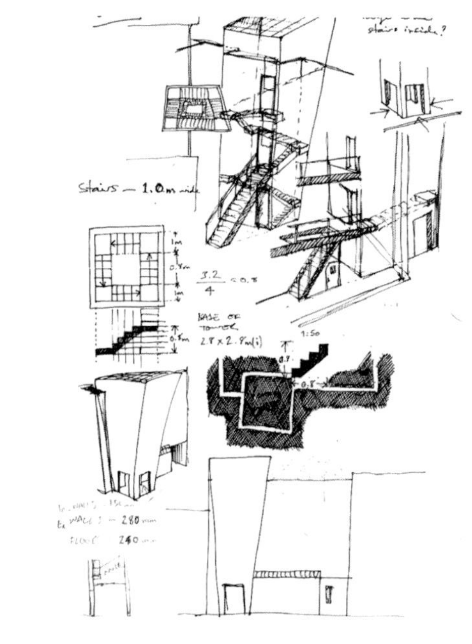

6

War zone → Bad weather → Noisy, Black, → Hide
Good weather → Silent, Calm, Bright → emerge
staircase,
the passage between floors is like a boundary
to cross a boundary we need to be challenged,
→ create a staircase that is mentally challengin
→ Zaha Hadid as president
SWEET TEMPTERESS

THE IDEA IS KEY

Anyone can sketch, it's easy to manipulate lines on paper. The importance is the sophistication of the idea behind the line and the thinking that stimulates it. Accuracy or even technical skill aren't the primary considerations here, it's the idea. Leonardo da Vinci, for example, used sketches to analyse the human body, to better understand the mechanics of muscles and the structure of the skeleton. He used his sketches to inform his subsequent designs of machines and architecture.

The sketch is a loose drawing, and as such it can be reworked and redirected to explore different possibilities. A sketch can be of a fantastically impossible idea, something futuristic or surreal, or it can outline the details of a concept and how these are applied to a piece of architecture. Sketching allows the exploration of an idea, a testing of possibilities. Only when the idea exists on paper in sketch form, can it be further developed.

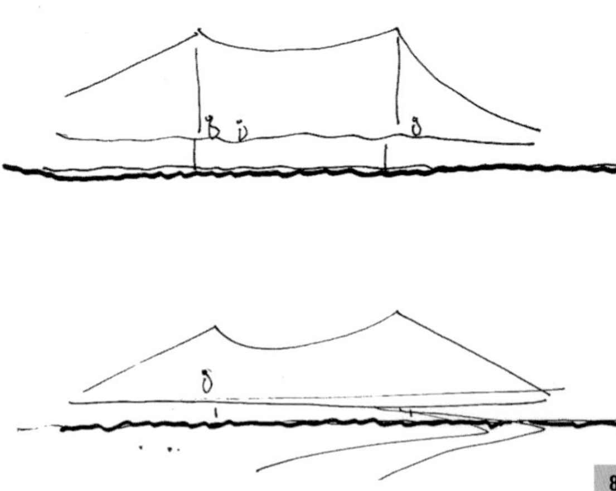

CONCEPTUAL SKETCHES

Conceptual sketches are created the moment that an architectural idea is conceived. These sketches connect idea with architecture. They can be abstract, metaphorical or even a formalised doodle that allows the journey of thinking to develop.

Oscar Niemeyer b.1907

A Brazilian architect, Niemeyer was a teacher and practitioner of architecture. He is most renowned for his cultural buildings for the United Nations in New York (1947) and a range of government buildings in Brazil. He uses dramatic forms at the scale of the city to produce a monumental architecture.

7. Serpentine Gallery Pavilion
Oscar Niemeyer, 2003
This pavilion was built as a temporary structure for the Serpentine Gallery in London. It was designed as a light and open structure that was linked to the park by a ramp. The pavilion took a simple structural form, appearing almost as if it were floating on the landscape.

8. Concept Sketches of Niemeyer's Serpentine Gallery Pavilion
These sketches of the same pavilion demonstrate the basic concept that underpins the architectural form.

9. & 10. Analytical sketches
Analytical sketches deconstruct an idea in order to allow a better understanding of the development and assembly behind it. Both of these analytical sketches investigate ideas of stairs and spaces.

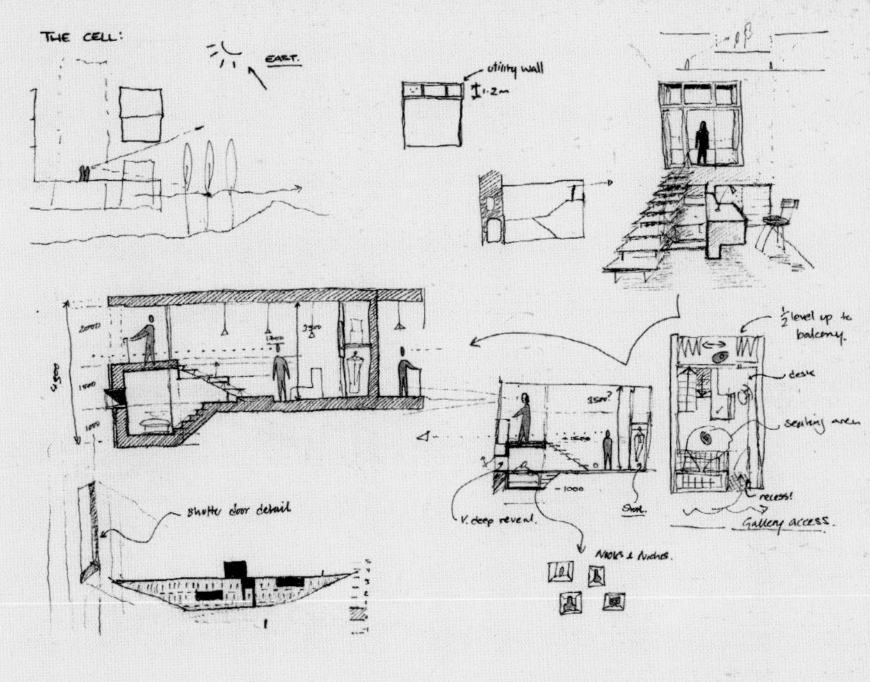

Analytical sketches take an idea and examine it in detail, usually as part of a series of steps to explain why something is the way it is, or how it will eventually be. Analytical sketches allow the deconstruction of an idea. Spaces can be analysed in terms of the activities or functions that will occur within them and cities can be analysed in terms of the experiences, journeys or building mass they contain.

Buildings can be specifically analysed in terms of measurables such as the amount of light in, or the function of, its different rooms and spaces. Such analysis is central to understanding the present condition, so that it can be responded to through the architectural idea or proposition. This analysis needs to be concise and diagrammatically clear.

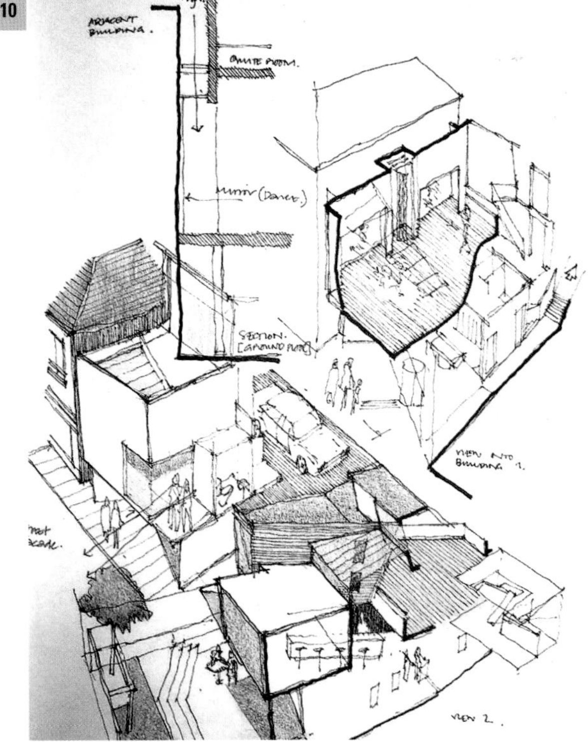

11

OBSERVATIONAL SKETCHES

Some of the best ideas come from acquiring a better understanding of something that already exists. Observational sketches can reveal details of form and structure that help provide better understanding. This type of sketching can be likened to life drawing; by drawing the body the artist develops a greater understanding of it, both proportionally and mechanically. The same process can be applied to drawing a building; doing so allows the exploration of its individual components and an awareness of how they relate to the whole. For example, the details of how different materials are juxtaposed and join together can reveal expressive or implicit architectural ideas.

12

11. Observational Sketches of the San Benedict Chapel
The San Benedict Chapel in Switzerland is explored and described here through observational sketches. The interior sketch (top) describes a personal interpretation of the light entering the chapel.

12. San Benedict Chapel (interior [top] and exterior [below]), Graubünden, Switzerland
Peter Zumthor, 1987–1989
These photographs show the chapel's elevation and the light entering its interior space. Compare these to the sketches.

13

14

SKETCHBOOKS: CONTAINERS OF IDEAS

Sketchbooks represent a collection of ideas and different journeys of exploration and understanding. They are emotional, raw and bursting with potential. An architect's sketchbook allows an idea to be taken and pursued beyond reality, sometimes in the wrong direction, until there is no mileage left in it. At other times it explores concepts that start as two-dimensional, raw sketches and finish as a realised building; the leap of ambition can be enormous!

Sketchbooks contain visual notes to stimulate and inform. This form of notetaking is developed through observation of real situations (understanding how buildings are) as well as theoretical explorations (why buildings are).

The process of developing an architectural idea can be well documented and recorded in a sketchbook, but this works in conjunction with the computer in the communication of architectural design. What starts as a concept sketch is then drawn to scale on a computer. Parts of this drawing can then be further analysed and redesigned in the sketchbook, before being developed as a finished proposal on the computer. The computer and the sketchbook represent the two diverse types of thinking that are needed for architecture; the sketchbook is imaginative and intuitive, and the computer defined and precise.

13. & 14. Perspective Sketches
These drawings explore the way in which light enters the San Benedict Chapel. The use of colour on these perspective sketches creates an animated and realistic impression of the internal space.

Scale

Scale is a critical consideration in architectural and spatial design as it allows the comparison of a drawing or model of an architectural idea to its real-size representation. Scale is the relative representation of an idea to a measurement, or system of measurement, that is universally known or understood.

Understanding a scale system allows the idea of a specific space to be properly communicated. Aligning the idea to something that we understand the scale of will help us to better understand the proportions of a concept. For example, a person placed in a room or building is something we can immediately connect with in terms of scale. Similarly, a piece of furniture, such as a bed or chair, also relates to human scale and so again its placement within a room will help our understanding of architectural concepts, proportions and spaces.

Scale is one of the first notions we need to understand in order to start designing structures for people to inhabit, because it allows us to comprehend how we can physically occupy a space – whether it is intended to be a tight, intimate and close space, or a loose, large and open one.

The Powers of Ten

Scale needs to be understood in both a physical and a relative sense. 'The Powers of Ten' (1968), a film by Charles and Ray Eames, is an important study of scale. This film opens with a shot of a person lying on a picnic mat. The viewer can easily comprehend the recognisable scale of this as it is full-size or 1:1 ratio. The film then moves each frame by a power of ten, first to 1:10 (one tenth real size), and then 1:100 (one hundredth real size) and so on until the scale reaches the (then) knowledge of the universe.

This film provides a useful way to understand the relative nature of scale. Understanding scale necessitates an understanding of the actual or real size of objects as well as the perceived and represented size of objects. Scale is a concept of imagining spaces, objects or buildings at different levels of detail.

For more information visit www.powersof10.com

15. Scale Models (shown left to right: 1:2000, 1:200 and 1:20)
These models are produced at a range of scales, each is increasing in scale by a factor of 10. Each incremental increase in scale allows more detail to be understood.

Scale Ratio	Application
1:1 Full Size	Details of furniture and materials
1:2	Details of furniture and materials
1:5	Buildings
1:10	Building and interior details
1:20	Building and interior details
1:50	Interior details and small building plans
1:100	Overall larger building plans
1:200	Overall larger building plans and site layouts
1:500	Site layouts and context relationship
1:1000	Surrounding landscape and site location
1:1250	Map scale location
1:2500	Large map scale location

15

Scale of 1:2000

Scale of 1:200

Scale of 1:20

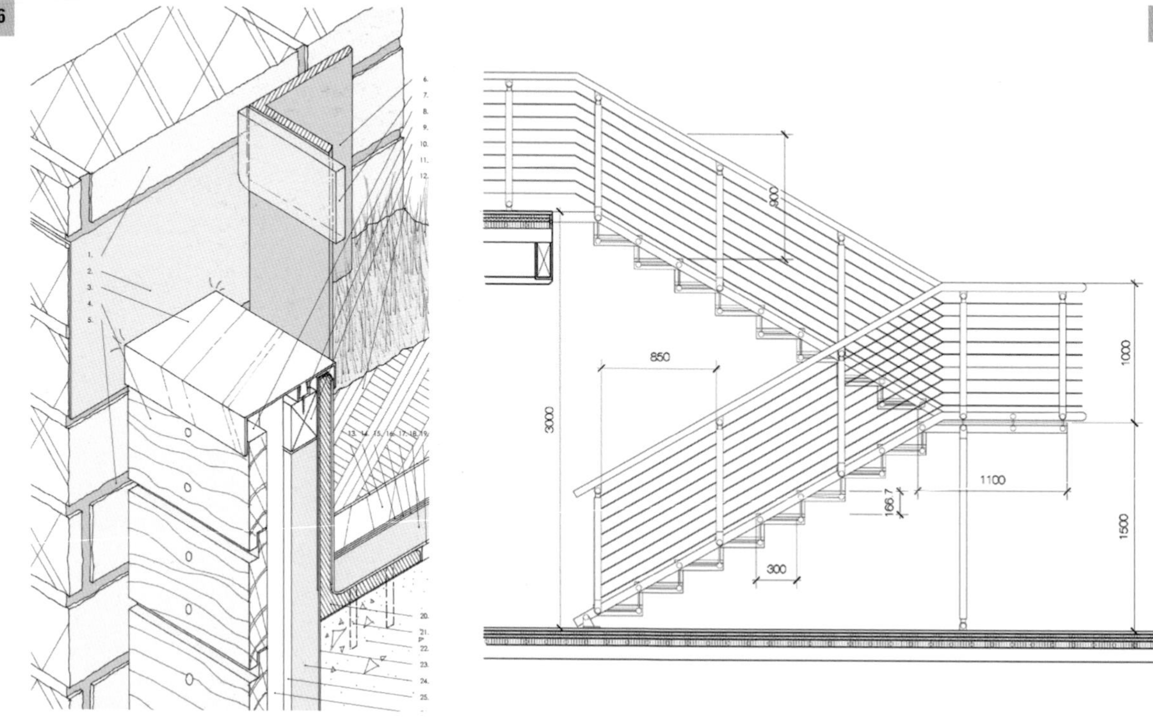

APPROPRIATE SCALE

Appropriateness of scale, using the correct ratio to explain the information effectively, is crucial as it affects the communication and understanding of a concept. Architects use different scales than those used by engineers or other designers.

The first scale ratio to understand is 1:1 or full-size scale, which is real or actual size and is used in architecture for designing small components and conducting smaller investigations of space. Sometimes spaces can be mocked up at real scale, much like a stage set, to investigate a concept. All scale ratios are expressed proportionately to full-size scale.

After 1:1, each scale ratio is used in different contexts to allow varying aspects or details of an idea to be drawn and expressed.

Construction details are expressed as 1:5 or 1:10 scale, Such details are usually concerned with understanding junctions in buildings, for example, where walls meet the floor and the roofs or the foundations.

The next range of scale, 1:20 and 1:50, are traditionally used to understand the interior aspects of rooms and layouts or to communicate a larger idea of construction and structure.

Building layouts are explored at 1:50, 1:100 and 1:200 depending on the size of the structure. Site relationships are drawn at scale ratios of 1:100, 1:200 and 1:500. The largest scale drawings are maps that indicate site location, and these are usually produced at ratios of 1:1000, 1:1250 or 1:2500.

18

19

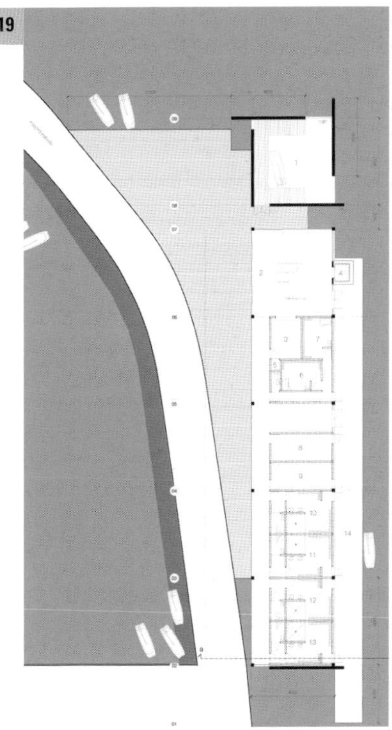

16. 1:5 Isometric Scale Drawing
This is a scale drawing of a construction detail.

17. 1:10 Scale Section Drawing
This is a cross-section, scale drawing of a staircase.

18. 1:50 Scale Plan
This drawing indicates the internal layout of an apartment.

19. 1:100 Scale Plan
This scale drawing shows a building in the context of its relationship to site.

20. 1:2500 Scale Urban Layout
This large-scale map shows a site location.

20

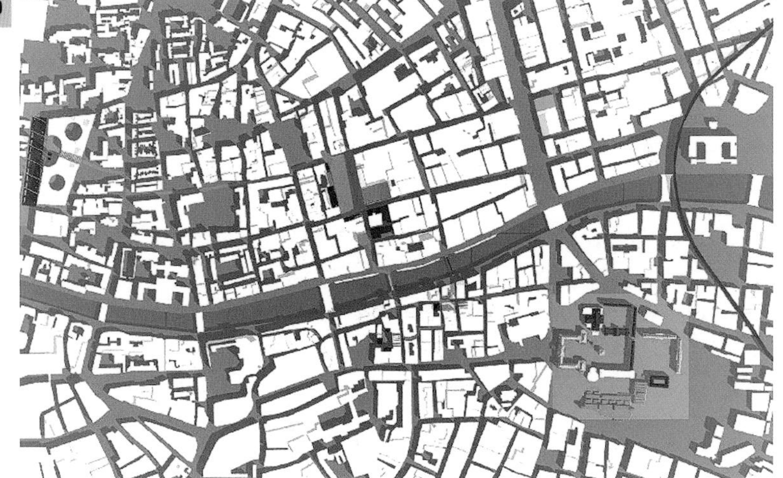

Orthographic Projection

Orthographic projection is a means of representing a three-dimensional object in two dimensions. In architecture, orthographic projection generally takes one of three forms: plan, section and elevation drawings.

A **plan** is an imagined horizontal cross section of a room or building 1.2 metres above ground or finished floor level. A **section** drawing shows a vertical cross section of a building or space. The **elevation** drawing displays the building's outside wrapping; its face or façade.

All these types of drawings are measured; they each use scale to communicate the spaces and forms contained within them. When architects refer to a 'full set' of drawings, this term encompasses plan, section, elevation and detail drawings. With the full set of information, and with each drawing type displayed at varying scales, a building design can be communicated clearly and understood as a three-dimensional proposition. It can be costed by a quantity surveyor, an engineer can see the architectural intention, and a builder can use the drawings to construct the building accurately. Independently each type of drawing communicates specific information, but collectively they explain the architecture completely.

PLANS

Plans need to explain the horizontal layers of the building; the basement (or below ground area), the ground floor, all other floor levels and the roof plan.

A site location plan is the first kind of drawing that explains a building. It is usually a bird's eye view and shows the surrounding area, incorporating the entrance to the building and, importantly, a north point.

Plans can be selective and just show a single room, or be diagrammatic and display the whole building. The amount of detail in a plan can vary enormously. It may have furniture within it to show the scale and use of a space, or show the materials intended to be used for the interior, or it can simply display spaces, walls, windows and doors. A plan drawing will contain as much (or as little) information as is available at each stage of the design process.

21. Eccleston House Site Location Plan Drawing
John Pardey Architects, 2006

The site plan of this house explains the relationship of the building to its immediate context. The plan includes information about the surrounding landscape, available parking, orientation and the relationship of the house's rooms to external views and vistas. There is a clarity about the plan of the building when it is viewed in the context of its surrounding landscape.

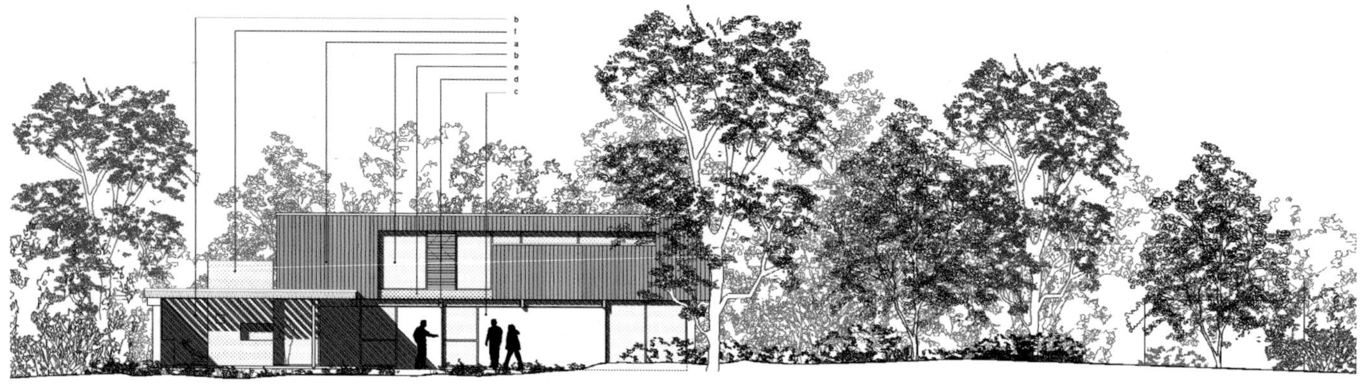

22

22. Eccleston House Elevation Drawing
John Pardey Architects, 2006
Context is described in an elevation drawing as it shows the building clearly in its environment. This elevation drawing gives us a sense of scale using figures and materials with shadow and colour. The trees provide a sense of scale to the building in relation to its surrounding landscape.

23. Eccleston House Final Presentation Plan
John Pardey Architects, 2006
This layout drawing showing the building's elevations describe the setting of the house in the context of its surroundings, a first floor plan and a range of perspective images. This provides a complete description of the scheme, from inside layout to the external form – as well as its relationship to its site.

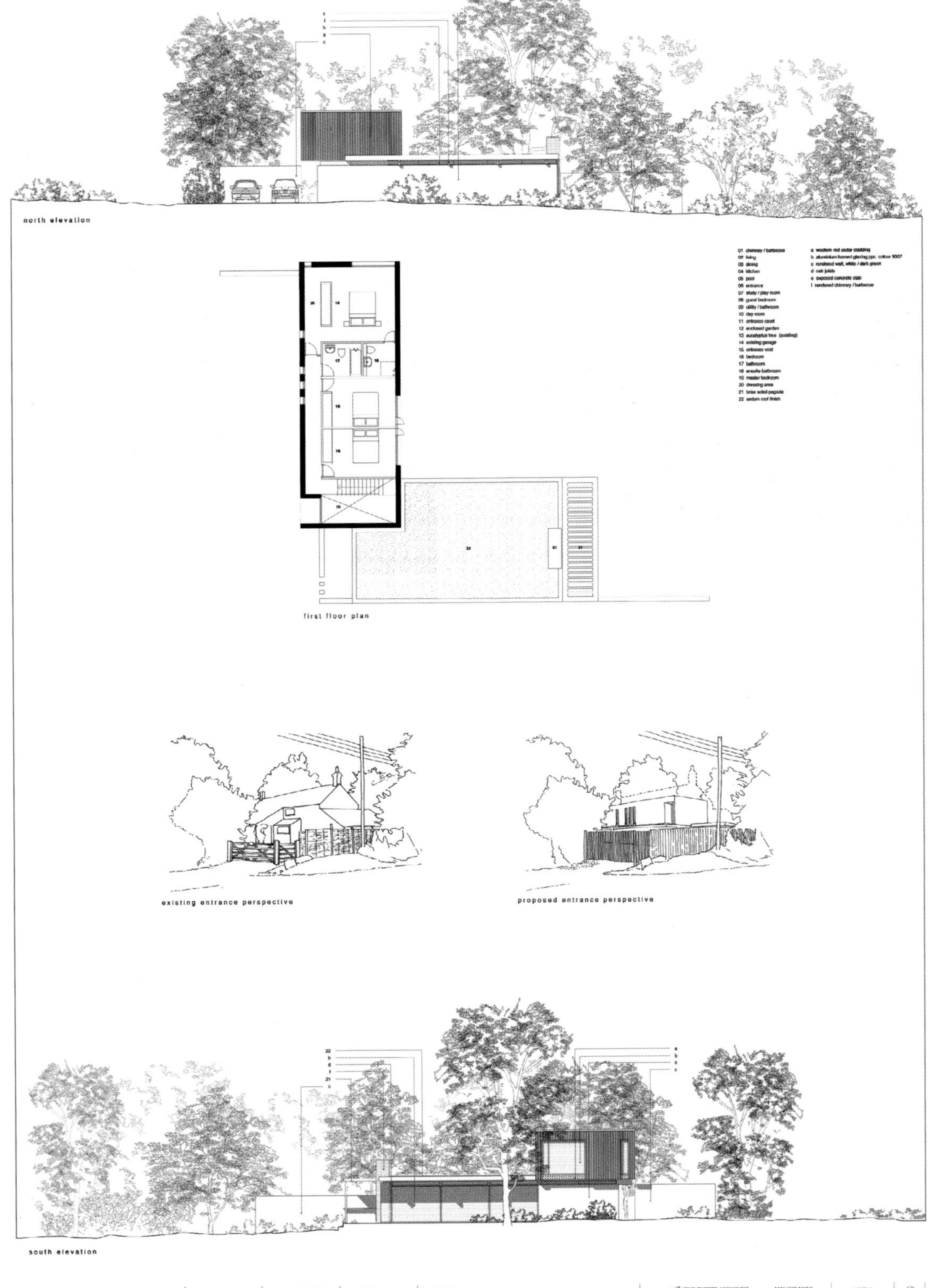
north elevation
01 chimney / barbecue
02 living
03 dining
04 kitchen
05 pool
06 entrance
07 study / play room
08 guest bedroom
09 utility / bathroom
10 day room
11 entrance court
12 enclosed garden
13 eucalyptus tree (existing)
14 existing garage
15 entrance void
16 bedroom
17 bathroom
18 ensuite bathroom
19 master bedroom
20 dressing area
21 brise soleil pagoda
22 sedum roof finish
a western red cedar cladding
b aluminium framed glazing ppc colour 9007
c rendered wall, white / dark green
d oak joists
e exposed concrete slab
f rendered chimney / barbecue
first floor plan
existing entrance perspective
proposed entrance perspective
south elevation
title: Proposed first floor plan, north + south elevation
status: planning
drawing no: LCE - PP- 05
scale: 1:100
date: Oct 2005
project: Latchmore Corner
revision:
JOHN PARDEY ARCHITECTS

24

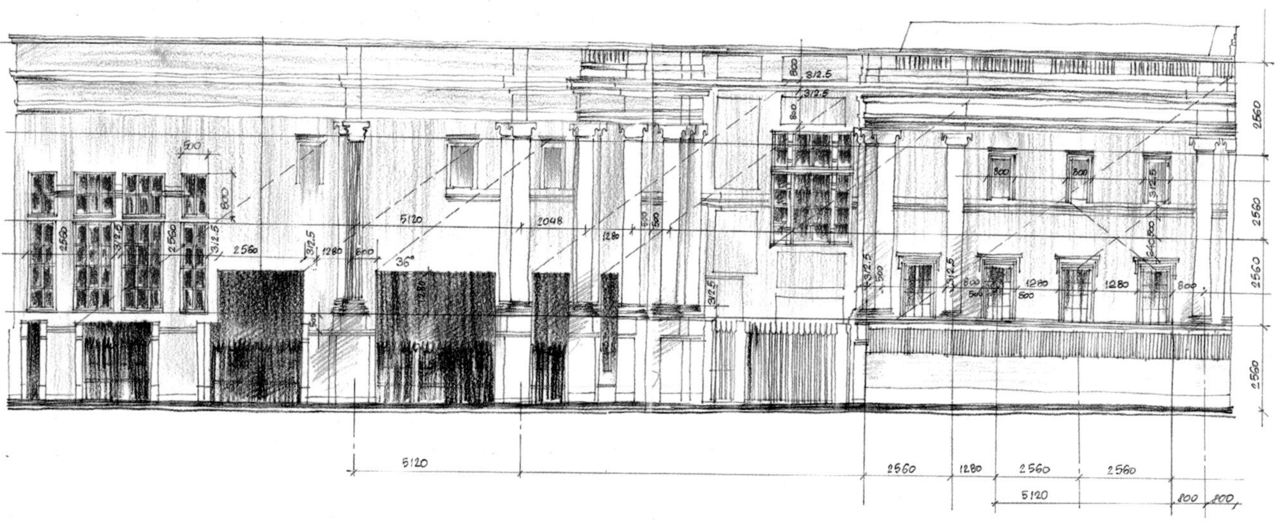

ELEVATION

Elevation drawings display a building's or structure's façade. Elevation drawings are usually created from the view of each direction that the building or site faces (the north-facing elevation or the west-facing elevation and so on). These drawings can provide a sense of depth by using tone to show where shadows may fall and in doing so affect the building or site. Elevation drawings are designed using mathematical precision, geometry and symmetry to determine the overall effect.

It is important to design and read an elevation drawing alongside a plan in order to develop an understanding of the 'bigger picture'. For example, the position of a window is important in terms of how a room functions, but the window also has to relate to the whole elevation and its composition. It is necessary for the architect to understand spaces and buildings at different scales and levels. In this example, the window relates to the room at one level and then to the street elevation at another.

24. Elevation Study
The measured survey dimensions on this elevation drawing explain how the various aspects of a street connect together visually. Shown in the form of an elevation, aspects of scale and proportion are also evident.

25. Section Drawings
These section drawings explain the relationship of the building to its surrounding landscape. The figures allow an understanding of scale and different levels of the architectural idea.

26. Elevation and Section Drawings of an Object
This is the side, or elevation, view of a shoe (left). Section drawings reveal the connection between the inside and outside. In this case the section drawing (right) reveals the shoe's internal structure and materiality.

25

Section 1

Section 2

A section drawing is an imagined 'slice' or cross section of a building or space. Section drawings impart an understanding of how spaces connect and interrelate with one another, and describe these relationships in a way that a plan can't. For example relationships between different interior spaces and floor levels can be revealed, or the connection between the inside and outside of a building can be seen.

26

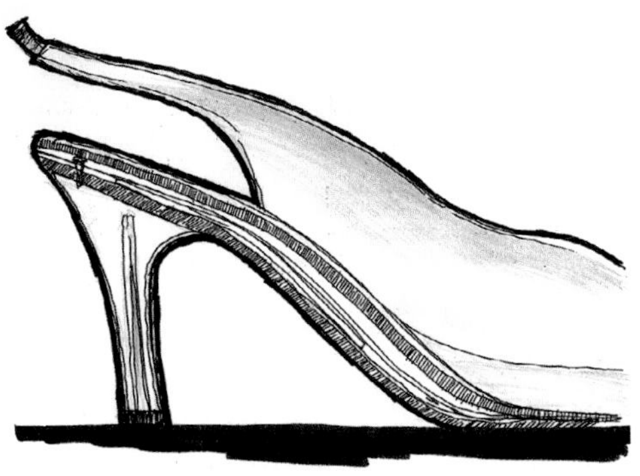

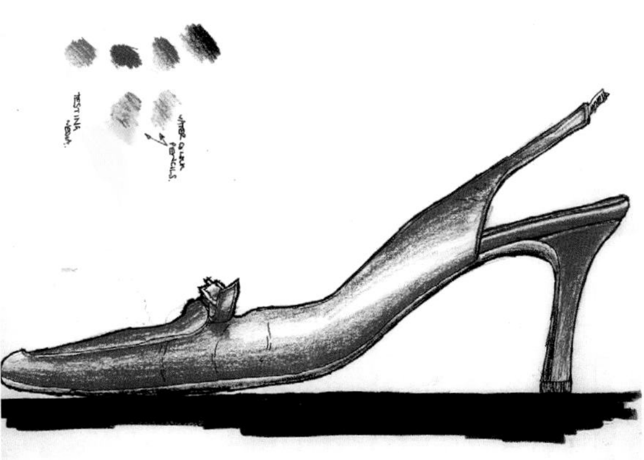

Perspective

Perspective drawings are very easily understood by those who cannot read plans as they are based on the idea of an individual's viewpoint (or perspective). They convey a 'real' impression or view of a space or place.

SKETCH PERSPECTIVE

To sketch in perspective is to try to create an impression of a 'real' view. To sketch in this way, the view first needs to be studied carefully and the point at which all the 'lines' of view appear to converge needs to be identified. This abstract point is called the vanishing point. This concept can be better understood by taking a photograph of a space and finding the point at which all the lines within it cross. This vanishing point is then used as a reference for the creation of perspective images.

Once the vanishing point is established, converging lines can be created to indicate the edges of surrounding elements, or in a room to distinguish horizontal planes (such as walls) from vertical planes (such as floors and ceilings). Other details can then be added to the image to further define the walls, windows or doors. With practice, perspective sketching is a skill that can be quickly acquired.

Constructed perspective drawing is more complex as it requires information from scale plan, section and elevations drawings.

Any perspective representation of a scene that includes parallel lines has one or more vanishing points. A one-point perspective drawing means that the drawing has a single vanishing point, usually directly opposite the viewer's eye and on the horizon. A two-point perspective drawing has parallel lines at two different angles. For example, looking at a house from the corner, one wall would recede towards one vanishing point and the other towards the opposite vanishing point. Three-point perspective is usually used for buildings seen from above or below.

Although constructed perspective drawings appear complex they do create interesting views of spaces and buildings.

27

28

29

27. & 28. Vanishing Point
These before and after images display the critical lines for creating a perspective. The solid line denotes the horizon and the broken lines denote all the lines of view, which converge at the vanishing point.

29. Sketch Perspective
This sketch demonstrates the idea of the 'vanishing point'; the image appears to disappear into the centre of the drawing. In reality, the walls of this street never get closer or meet, but to draw the perspective sketch convincingly, the illusion of a vanishing point must be applied.

Three-dimensional Images

Three-dimensional images communicate ideas that cannot be conveyed in two-dimensional plan, section and elevation drawings. Drawing in three dimensions gives depth to an image and makes it appear more realistic. Some three-dimensional drawings are sketched and others adopt a more measured approach. Axonometric and isometric three-dimensional drawings for example are geometrically constructed.

ISOMETRIC DRAWINGS

Isometric drawings produce three-dimensional images. In these drawings the length, width and height are represented by lines that are 120 degrees apart, with all measurements in the same scale.

To create this type of drawing, a plan, and section and elevation drawings (to scale) of the building or space are required. The plan drawing is then rotated so that it sits at 30 degrees to the horizontal or vertical plane. Placing a piece of tracing paper over the plan will then allow you to redraw the image at the new angle. Lines are then projected vertically from the corners of the redrawn plan; these will represent the height of the building or space. All the measurements are taken from the elevation or section drawings to obtain height, and vertical dimensions should then be transferred to the isometric drawing.

Distorting the plan at 30 degrees to the horizontal or vertical plane makes an isometric drawing more difficult to construct than an axonometric drawing (see page 110), as some initial manipulation is required.

Isometric drawings are useful to describe an internal space or series of larger spaces effectively and explain three-dimensional construction details and assembly drawings.

30

32

UNIT 201.5 A LITTLE HOUSE OF YOUR OWN
JAYNE BANNISTER JANUARY 2002

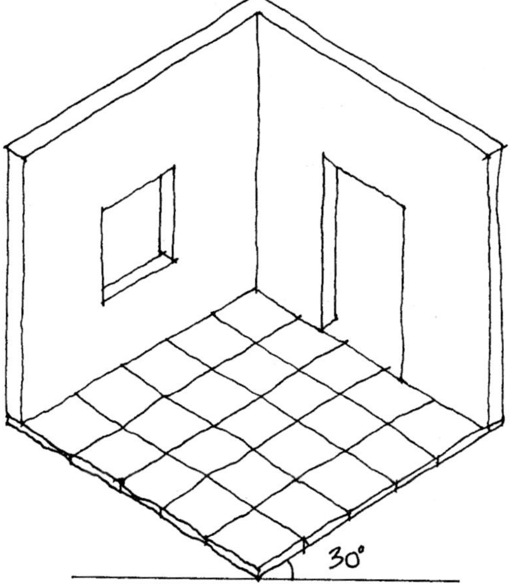

31

30. & 31. Isometric Drawings

Isometric images combine perspective (which gives a realistic impression of an image) with a three-dimensional view. If used as a series of drawings, they are a useful tool to describe how something is assembled or how component parts connect together.

32. Isometric Construction Diagram

This diagram indicates how an isometric drawing is produced by distorting the plan at 30 degrees from the horizontal plane. Once the plan has been redrawn at this angle the lines for walls are projected vertically.

33

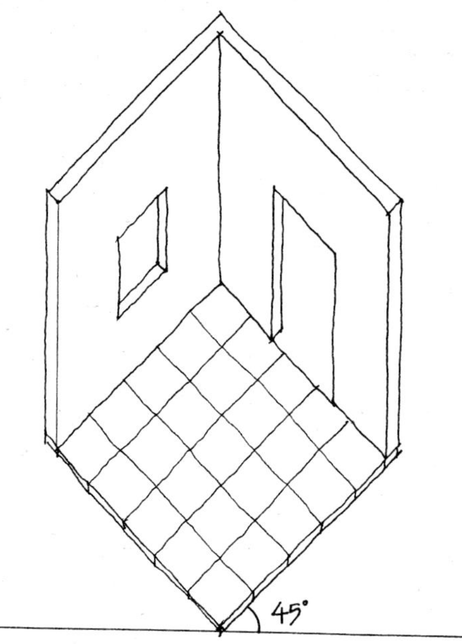

AXONOMETRIC DRAWINGS

An axonometric drawing creates a quick three-dimensional projection of a room or space and is produced from a plan drawing. Axonometric drawings are the simplest representational means of achieving a three-dimensional effect.

This type of drawing again requires plan, section and elevation drawings (to scale) of the building or space. The plan drawing is then rotated so that it sits at 45 degrees to the horizontal or vertical plane and is redrawn at this new angle. Using the same approach as with the isometric drawing, lines are then projected vertically from the corners of the redrawn plan and all measurements are taken from the elevation or section drawings and transferred to the axonometric drawing.

Axonometric drawings are quick to produce, but the resultant image, particularly if it is one of a building's exterior, can make the roof appear exaggerated.

Exploded views are a good way of showing detail. These are drawings that appear literally to have been taken apart, and exploded axonometric drawings will explain how a building can be deconstructed and reassembled.

33. Axonometric Construction Diagram
An axonometric drawing is created by redrawing the plan at an angle of 45 degrees from the horizontal or vertical plane. Once the plan has been redrawn in this manner the lines for walls are projected vertically.

34. Malevich's Tektonik, London
Zaha Hadid, 1976–1977
This axonometric drawing echoes the style of Malevich, a painter of the Russian Constructivist movement who used abstract drawings to create a series of compositions.

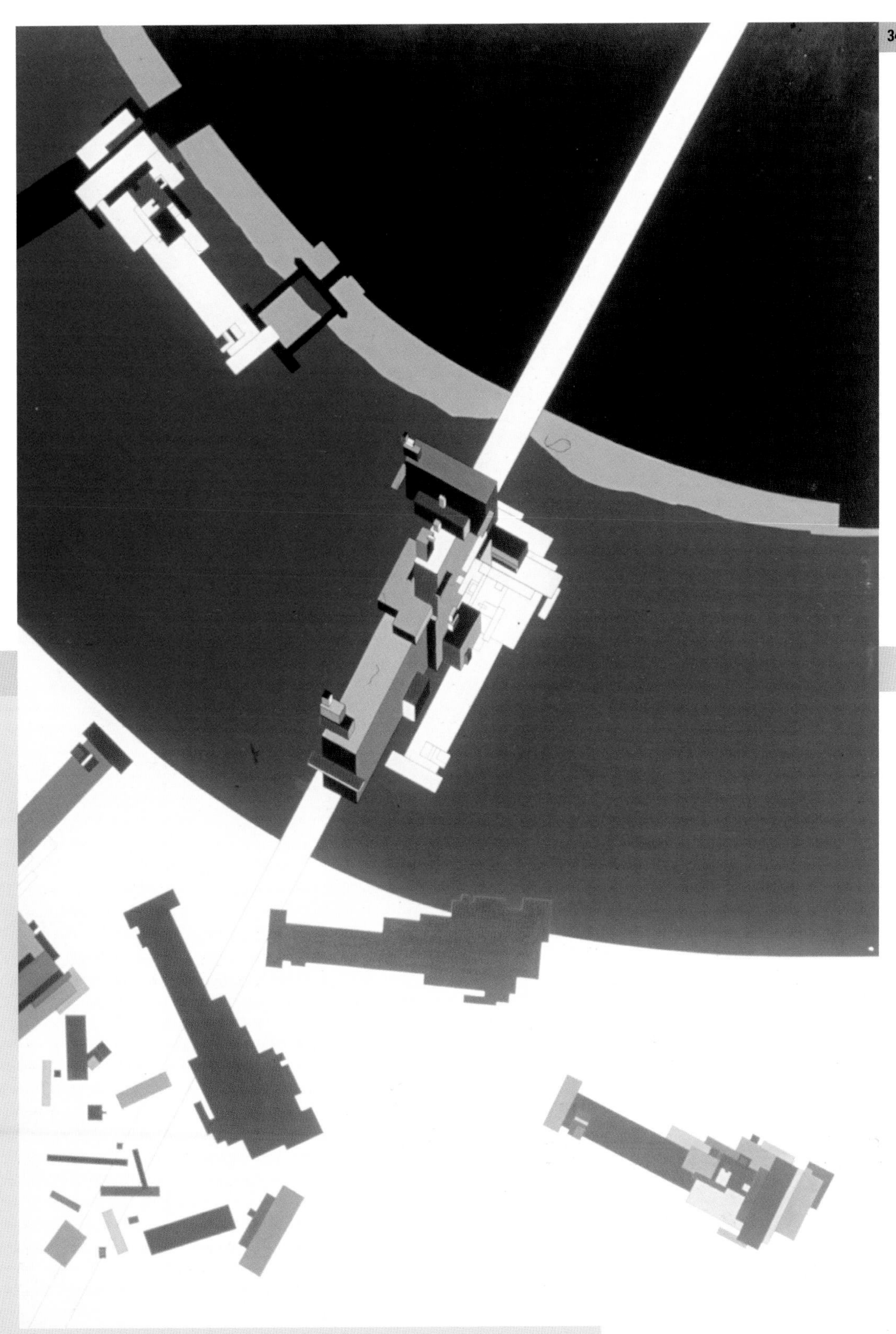

34

36

Physical Modelling

Physical models offer another means to show an idea in three-dimensional form. Physical models can take many forms, be made from a range of materials and exist at a variety of scales. Just like different drawing types, different model types are used at different stages of the design process to best explain a particular concept or idea.

34

35

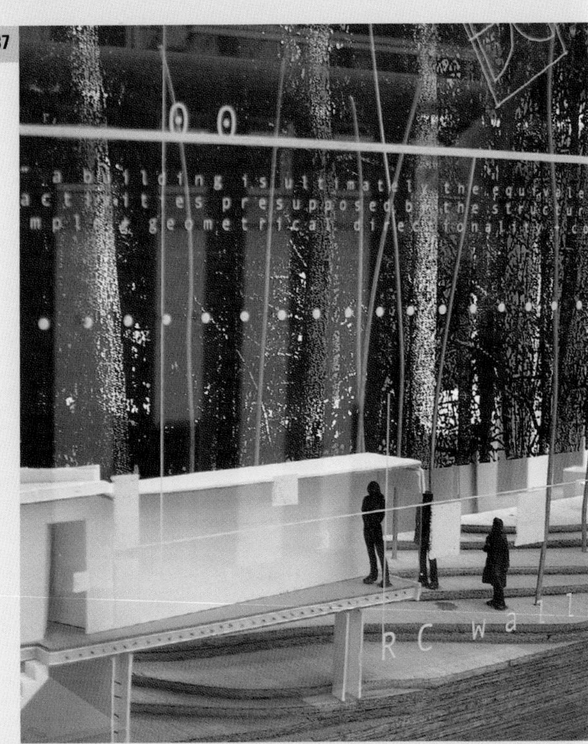

37

34. Sketch Model
These are quick developmental models made at the early stages of an idea. Sketch models allow changes to be considered, so the design can adapt.

35. An Urban Model
This model explains the context of the city surrounding the site, with roads, buildings and trees described. Also the relative heights of buildings can be understood.

36. A Finished Model
This is a model which shows the final idea of a building, sitting in its landscape. It contrasts with the site around it which remains white. The building has detail of windows, openings and roof to allow a complete understanding of the concept and its location.

37. A Detail Model
This model is exploring the relationship between the building and the landscape, the interior and the exterior of an idea. A sheet of perspex shows a slice through the building.

Different types of physical models are used at different stages of a project's development. In all model types the important issues for consideration are the scale of the model and the materials used to describe the idea. It is not necessary to use the actual intended materials for the project, it is sufficient to just suggest finishes in various ways. However, sometimes using the intended material for the build, such as wood or clay, in the model can strongly communicate the design concept.

Sketch models are quick to construct. They may be produced to scale, or at earlier stages of a project, in a more abstract form, exploring an idea of materials that might be used or a site concept. Sketch models allow the architect to quickly develop a spatial idea.

Concept models use various materials to produce an exaggerated interpretation of an idea or concept. Concept models can be produced at a range of scales and are especially useful at the start of a scheme to explain the direction of the idea. As such the information they contain needs to be concise and clear.

Detail models explore a specific aspect of an idea, this may be how materials come together at a construction junction or perhaps an interior detail of the finished build. The focus in a detail model is on a single element, not the whole building or architectural concept.

Urban models provide an understanding of a site in the context of its surrounding location. In this type of model the detail is not critical, but the overview is. Urban models provide information about the location of key site elements and the site's topography. The relative position and scale of these elements are important considerations here.

Finished models describe the final architectural idea, and the attention to detail in these models is crucial. Finished models may have roofs or walls that can be removed to describe important aspects of the interior space.

CAD Modelling

CAD modelling combines aspects of two- and three-dimensional imaging. CAD software is sufficiently sophisticated to be used at different stages of the design process, from the initial thinking to on-site detailing and implementation. Many software programs require the plan and elevation data in order to produce an accurate set of images. This data is usually a series of coordinates or the length and height measurements of walls with specific parameters.

Computer Aided Design (CAD) has made many aspects of building design more efficient. Ideas and drawings can be quickly rendered, revisited, manipulated and revised. Many CAD models allow quick interaction with the viewer and a building can be explored with 'fly throughs' allowing the viewer to take journeys through the schemes and interact with models of the buildings.

There are many software packages, such as AutoCAD, RealCAD or SolidWorks, which allow the design of elements such as furniture or construction components in two- and three-dimensional forms. Other specialist software allows for the design of buildings and three-dimensional manipulation of the spaces within them. Entire cities can also be designed and visualised using CAD software, allowing an understanding of placing a building on a particular site or location and the impact it may have on adjacent sites.

Rendering packages can provide impressions of realistic material finishes. Other software can help measure and design aspects of shadow, lighting, insulation, structural performance and building energy performance. Each stage of the design process has different specialist programs that can assist with the development and testing of the design idea. Using many of these programs together can provide useful ways to explore a design idea or create a presentation of the complete architectural concept and experience.

38. Pool Competition
David Mathias and Peter Williams, 2006
This CAD image was generated for a swimming-pool scheme and uses computer graphics to create a dynamic effect.

39. CAD Perspective
David Mathias and Peter Williams
Perspective views such as this one can be generated and manipulated quickly and effectively with CAD software. The image collages CAD graphics with on-site photographs.

38

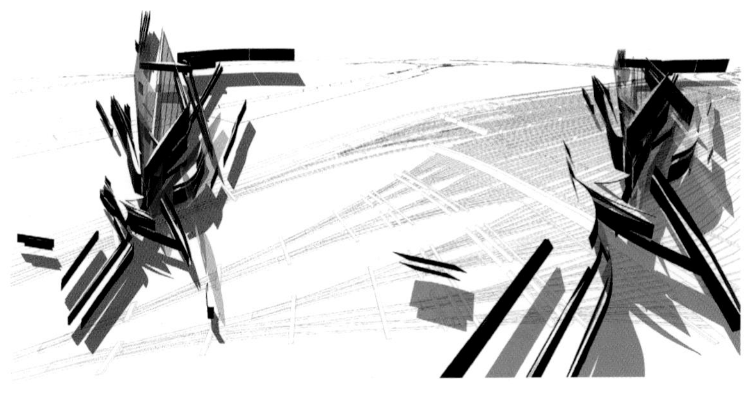

39

Layout and Presentation

Standard paper sizes determine the size of drawings in a portfolio. In Europe the ISO (International Organisation for Standardisation) system is used, and this gives a sense of uniformity to hard-copy presentations. In the ISO paper size system, the height-to-width ratio of all pages is the square root of two (1.4142 : 1). This value underpins the golden section and the Fibonacci sequence.

In terms of appropriate size of layout there are many factors to consider. Large-scale drawings may need more physical space to be presented, and drawings that need to make an impact may also need to be displayed at a large scale. A smaller-scale drawing will of course be physically smaller and so require less drawing space.

It is critical that the drawing size comfortably accommodates the image at the appropriate scale. Key factors for layout selection are the actual drawing scale, the intended audience for, or reader of, the drawing, the clarity of the written information that supports the drawing (such as its title, legend scale, and north point, which is essential on a plan), and the requirement that the size of this supporting information does not distract the reader or viewer from the drawing.

Portrait or landscape layout is another consideration. This choice must relate to other drawings (if the presentation is one of a series of images), and how the format helps the information to be easily read and better understood.

The Fibonacci Sequence

0, 1, 1, 2, 3, 5, 8, 13, 21, 34, 55, 89, 144, 23

To Create a Golden Section

1. Take a square

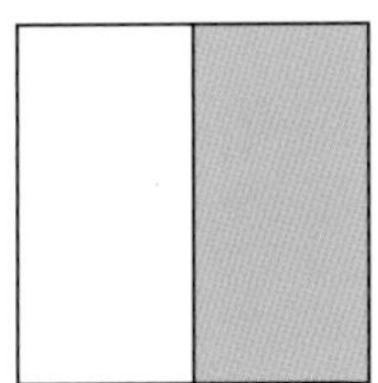

2. Dissect it

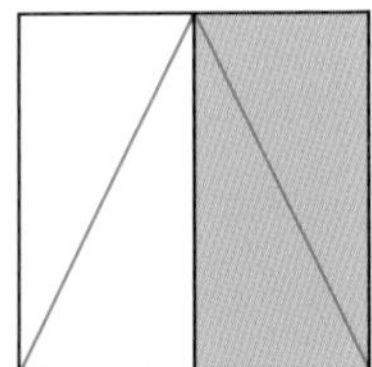

3. Form an isosceles triangle

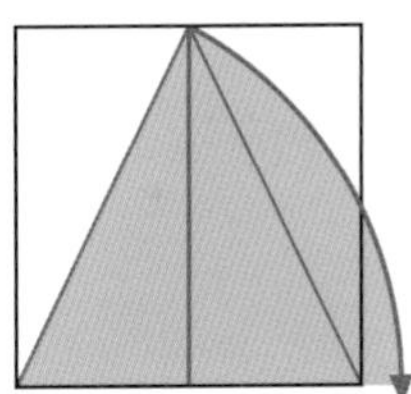

4. Extend an arc from the apex of the triangle to the baseline

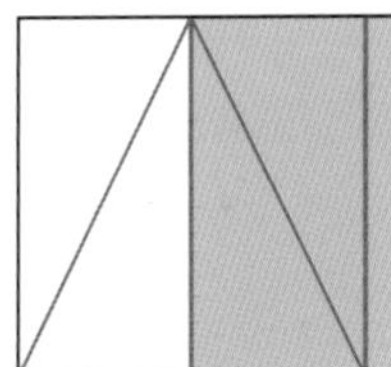

5. Draw a line perpendicular from the point at which the arc intersects it, and complete the rectangle

The Golden Section

The golden section is an irrational number, approximately 1.618, which possesses many interesting properties. Shapes defined by the golden section have long been considered aesthetically pleasing in Western cultures, reflecting nature's balance between symmetry and asymmetry and the ancient Pythagorean belief that reality is a numerical reality. Some studies of the Acropolis, including the Parthenon, conclude that many of its proportions approximate the golden ratio. The Parthenon's façade can be circumscribed by golden rectangles.

Fibonacci Numbers

Fibonacci, also known as Leonardo of Pisa, was born in Pisa, Italy (c. 1175). He has been described as a mathematical genius of number theory. He developed the Fibonacci series, in which each consecutive number is the sum of the two preceding numbers (1, 2, 3, 5, 8, 13, 21, 34, 55, 89, 144, etc.). As the series progresses, the ratio of a Fibonacci number divided by the immediately preceding number comes closer and closer to 1.618, the golden section.

377, 610, 987, 1597, 2584, 4181, 6765, 10946

Storyboarding

Storyboarding is a technique often used by film makers and animators, which can also be used by architects to communicate a plan for a design idea. The storyboard is a very useful tool for designers as it uses captions and incorporates comments and spaces to suggest scenes and activities. The storyboard is a two-dimensional representation of space and time.

Storyboards are used in film making to create layouts for scenes, bringing together the story, script and location as a plan for the narrative.

Usually the structure or framework for a storyboard is a series of boxes, which are filled with sketches to describe the characters and events in the narrative. In addition notes surround these loose sketches, which give further detail about the scene. This level of detail may describe movement or action and contain more information about the surrounding physical environment. The connection between each frame is also important, because it is these connections that bind the story together.

Storyboarding can be a very useful technique for architects because it offers a means to explain how events may take place within their architecture over time. Using the building as a kind of backdrop where potential events might take place is a useful way to plan presentations and pitch architectural concepts and ideas as a kind of narrative or story.

40

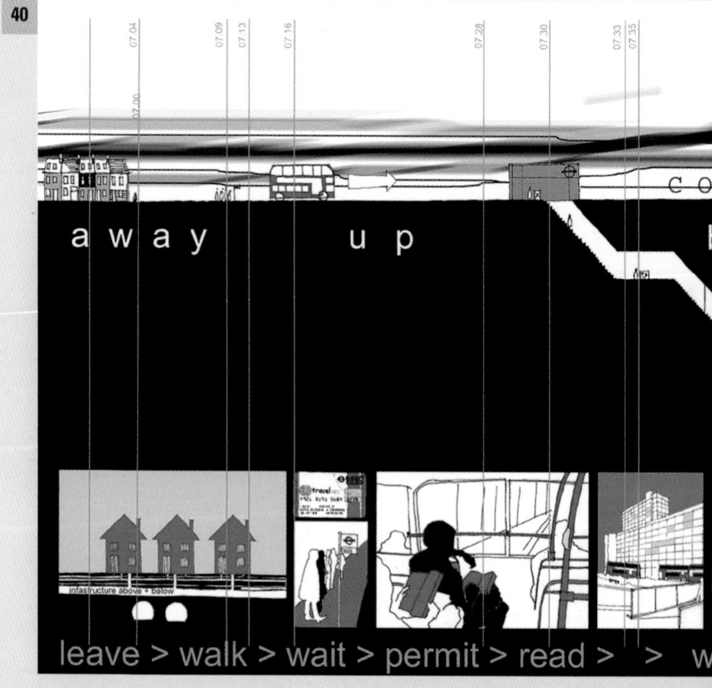

40. Storyboarding a Journey on the London Underground
Nicola Crowson, 2003
Here, a journey on the London Underground is described via a series of images, each one referring to different times and points along the journey's course. A storyboard can easily accommodate a series of images and help suggest a narrative or journey that unfolds over time.

Portfolios

A portfolio is a collection and record of work. For architects it must satisfy a specific range of requirements and is in itself a design 'project'. Portfolios can take several forms and need to contain a variety of representation techniques to fully explore and represent architectural ideas. They may incorporate sketches to explain concept, orthographic drawings (such as plans, sections and elevations), measured drawings, abstract images, photographs of physical models or CAD images. A portfolio is a kind of narrative that tells a story of your body of work, and before compiling any portfolio for viewing it is essential to know your intended audience.

PHYSICAL PORTFOLIOS

A physical portfolio is traditionally produced in an A1 (594 x 841 mm) format, although A3 (297 x 42 mm) portfolios are sometimes used for more concise presentations. However, the size of portfolio will be determined by the layout chosen and the intended audience.

Portfolios can be produced, revised and adapted for a range of purposes. An academic portfolio is a collection of work produced for a particular course. Professional portfolios may be used to present ideas to a client or to a prospective employer. Other portfolios may be more personal and allow presentation of a body of work or a particular project.

Whatever the intended audience or purpose of the portfolio, the information presented within it needs to be clear and the content edited and carefully planned. Often the portfolio may need to be seen without further supporting material (competition entries, for instance), and in such cases the need for clarity and accurate representation is crucial.

Tips for Preparing a Portfolio

1. Use a layout technique (such as storyboarding) to plan and organise your portfolio's content.
2. The orientation of the image sheets is very important. Remember a portfolio should read like a book, and sometimes double-page spreads (where two folio sheets read together as one) may be required.
3. Sequencing of drawings is important to accurately tell the story of the building or project from its conception through to final details.
4. The viewer should not have to move to read the work.

41

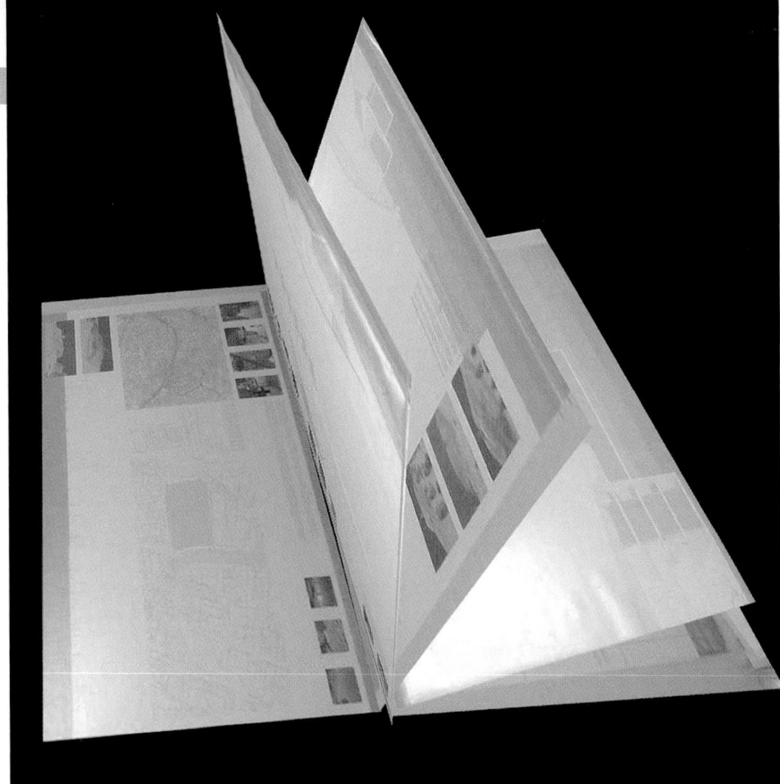

41. Student Portfolio

This is an A1 portfolio, which illustrates how two landscape sheets can connect when opened.

42. Portfolio Plan

The layout of a portfolio needs to be designed and the content organised in order to ensure that the body of work reads as a story, with a beginning, middle and end.

43. Storyboarding

Storyboarding can be used to plan a portfolio layout and provide an overview of the content. This is an outline layout that plans a portfolio as a series of logically progressing pages.

42

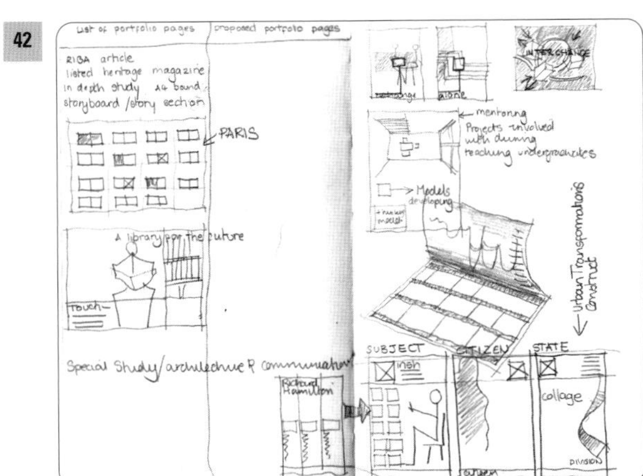

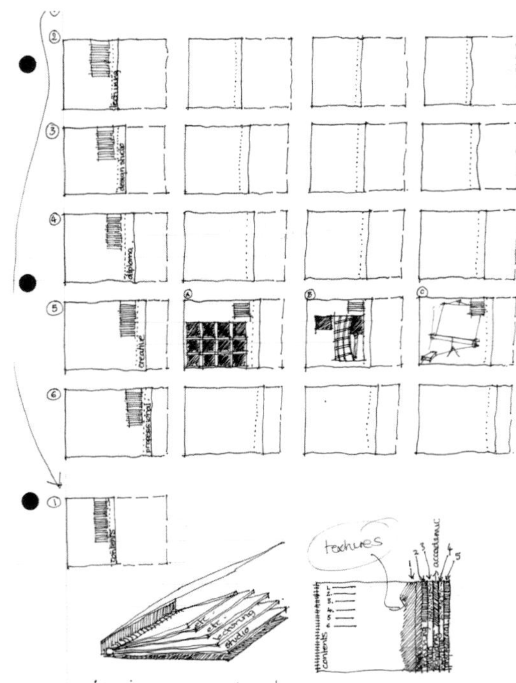

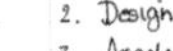

43

44

45

ELECTRONIC PORTFOLIO

Electronic portfolios, or e-portfolios, use digital means to produce a CD that can be projected or viewed on a computer. These portfolios are constructed using appropriate software (such as Microsoft's PowerPoint®, for example). To compile an electronic portfolio the images to be displayed must exist in digital form. This may mean that physical models need to be digitally photographed and enhanced and edited in PhotoShop, and drawings that originate in CAD software can again be edited for inclusion in an e-portfolio.

An important consideration here is the means of display for such a collection of images. Are they to be viewed on a computer screen or projected at a much larger scale? The quality, resolution and size of the images will need to be adjusted according to the audience and the way in which the audience will view the material.

A web portfolio is shown via the internet so it can be viewed or downloaded remotely or by anyone with access to the web.

44. John Pardey Architects
www.johnpardeyarchitects.com
A range of thumbnail images describes the extent of projects that John Pardey Architects deliver, ranging from private houses to larger master planning schemes. Each thumbnail image is linked to a range of drawings that explain the project in more detail.

45. Design Engine Architects
www.designenginearchitects.co.uk
This web portfolio has a series of clear choices on the home page, identifying four key architectural projects.

46. Panter Hudspith Architects
www.panterhudspith.com
This site uses powerful images on each page, which are accompanied by clear descriptive text. A local index on the site helps the user to navigate through the range of practice projects.

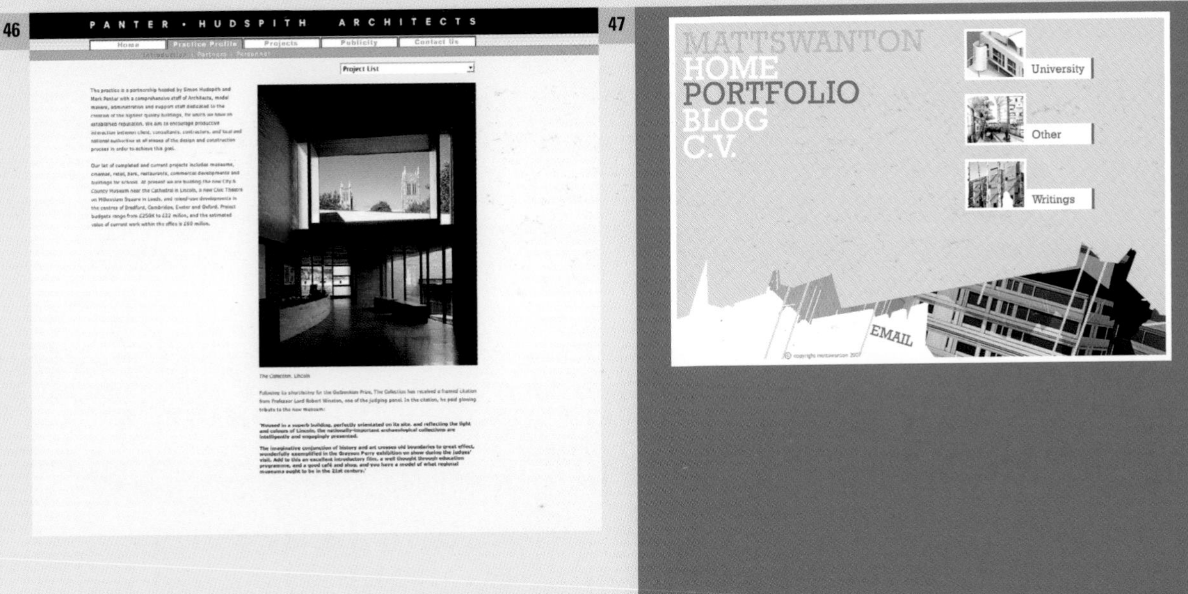

47. Matt Swanton
www.mattswanton.com
This personal website contains information from the architect's study and practice, as well as an array of experimental work. The site also includes a blog for users' comments and further discussion.

48. Make
www.makearchitects.com
Make use animated images on their website to create a powerful visual effect. Thumbnail rollover visuals connect the user to additional project information.

Chapter 5
Contemporary Ideas

Within the parameters of this book, contemporary ideas in architecture refer to those of the twentieth and twenty-first century. Architecture is heavily influenced by the zeitgeist (the spirit of the age), but when compared to other aspects of culture, such as art, design or technology, architecture is slower to react. It is not unusual for a large building or public monument to take a decade or longer to be conceived, developed and constructed. Even smaller, domestic-scale buildings, which are often indicative of the lifestyle and fashion of their time, aren't always immediate in their realisation.

1. Follydock Competition Rotterdam, The Netherlands
Lost Studio, 2006
Folly IFCR, the International Folly Contest Rotterdam, is a design competition for architects. The brief is to design an original folly in the context of the Rotterdam harbour area. As with many architectural competitions, the Follydock challenge offers the opportunity to stretch the boundaries of fantasy and reality.

This series of perspective views describes Lost Studio's competition entry. It is a set of floating balloons in the form of shipping containers, tied to existing shipping containers on the dockside.

1

Universal Ideas and Principles

There are universal ideas and concepts that transcend style or time and affect all architecture in varying ways. These have been categorised into three groups: geometry, form and route. Within each of these groups most architecture can be defined or described.

GEOMETRY

In this context, geometry describes the ordering and organising of spaces according to geometric principles. Geometry can affect the plan, elevation or section of a building, as well as its individual elements, such as the doors or windows.

Symmetry is an organising system that reflects either a plan, or elevation around a central line or axis. An axis connects two or more defined points and can regulate elements such as windows and doors (which will affect experiences such as views and vistas, and the entrance to and exit from buildings).

Proportion describes the relationship of parts to a whole. Within architecture proportion is the relationship of scale (see page 96) and the hierarchy of a building or structure's elements to its whole form.

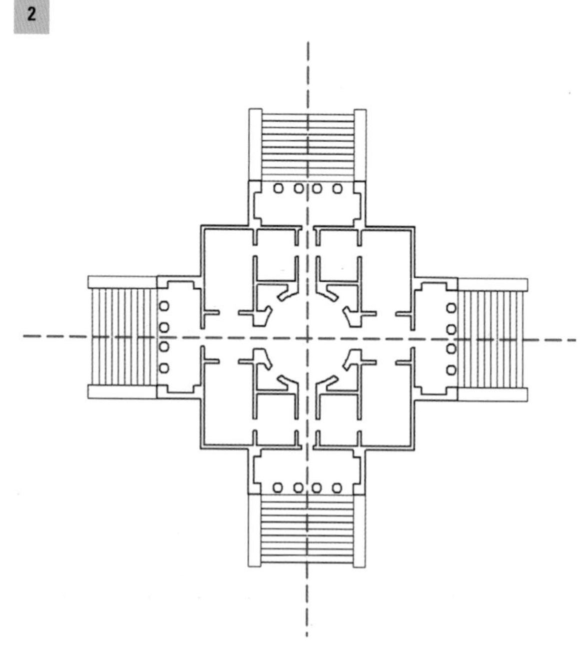

2. Plan of The Villa Rotunda
Symmetry in architecture symbolises rational mathematical principles. Plans for Andrea Palladio's Villa Rotunda (situated in Vincenza, Italy) show bilateral symmetry in two directions. The red lines indicate the axis of symmetry that crosses the villa's central point.

3

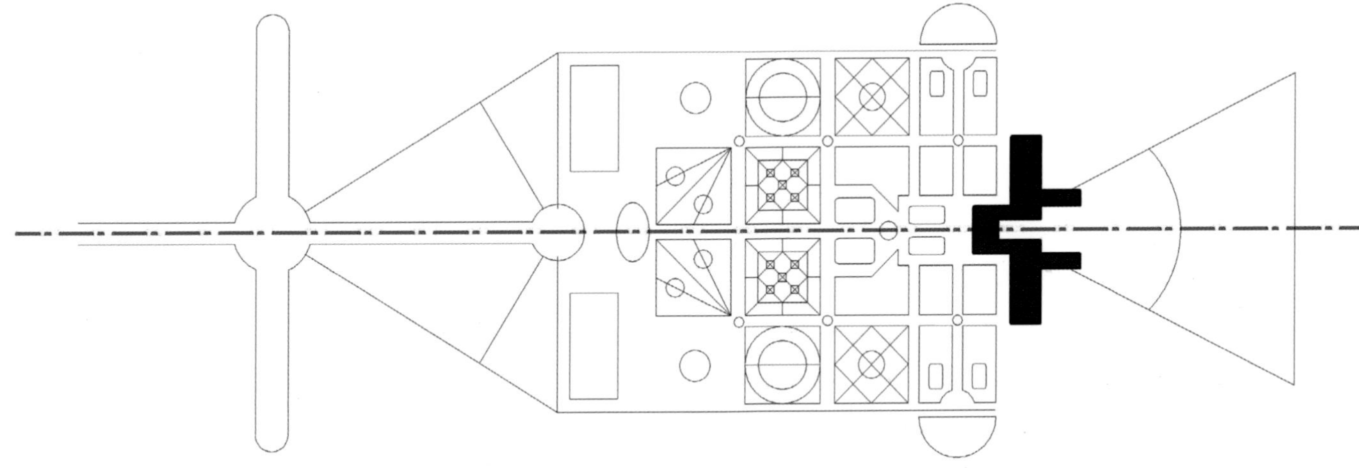

4

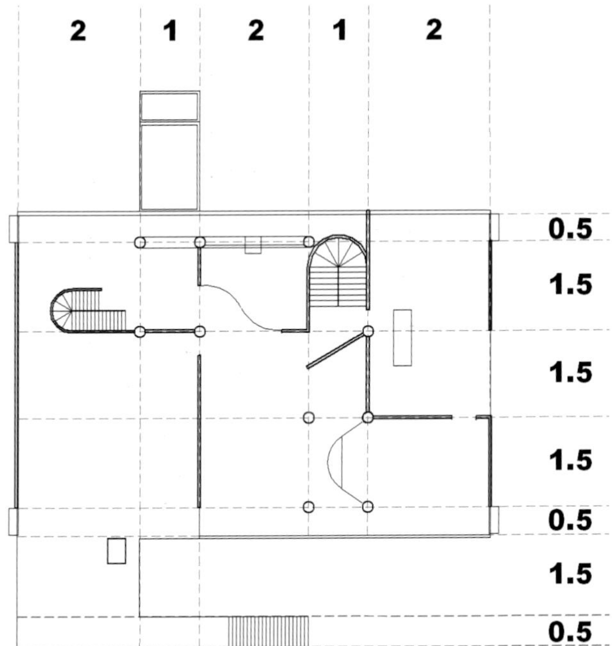

3. Plan of the Château de Versailles

This plan of the Château de Versailles displays the relationship of the château (designed by architect Louis Le Vau) to the gardens (designed by landscape architect André Le Notre) and demonstrates strong systems of symmetry along an axis. Within each of the parterre gardens other symmetrical patterns exist. The red lines here indicate the main organising axis of both garden and house.

4. Plan of Villa Stein

The seemingly irregular plan of Le Corbusier's Villa Stein (situated in Garches, France) is governed by the precise geometric proportioning system of a modular grid. The numbers shown relate to the module measurement that is applied to both the plan and the elevation of the building, which creates a certain rhythm.

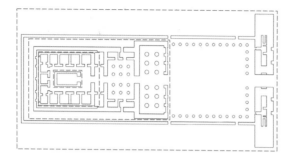

5

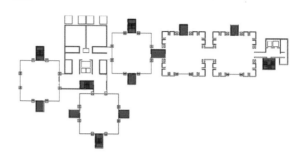

6

5. Plan of the Temple of Horus
This Egyptian temple, whose design is attributed to Ptolemy III and dates from 237–57 BC, consists of an inner sanctuary that is surrounded by a series of wrapping walls and colonnaded entrance courtyards and halls. The plan of the building reads as a series of layers around the central protected space.

6. Plan of Richards Medical Centre Philadelphia
One of Louis Kahn's principal ideas was the distinction between 'served' and 'servant' spaces. The Richards Medical Centre in Philadelphia, US, exemplifies this ideal. The glass-walled workrooms are 'served' by separate, freestanding brick chimneys. Each 'served' space has an independent structural frame with a complete set of supports and its own source of natural illumination.

FORM

Architectural concepts can be expressed using simple terms that characterise the form or shape of a building. Some forms are dynamic, sculptural and strongly influenced by the external appearance of the building. This category of design idea is described as 'function following form'. Other building forms are more practical, determined by the internal activities or purpose of the building. These ideas can be described as those of 'form following function'.

'Servant served' is a description that **Louis Kahn** used to describe the different categories of space in a building, be it a small-scale house or a large-scale civic building. Servant spaces have functional use, such as storage rooms, bathrooms or kitchens – the spaces that are essential for a building to function properly. Served spaces might be living or dining rooms or offices – spaces that the servant areas serve. This concept provides a very useful way to understand the organisation of a building.

Louis Kahn 1901–1974

Originally from Estonia, Kahn grew up in New York but he remained influenced by European classical architecture. Kahn was very interested in materials and their relationship to form, and was fascinated by the notions of served and servant spaces and the hierarchies in building plans.

His most important buildings are the Yale Art Gallery in Connecticut, US, the Richards Medical Centre in Philadelphia, US, the Kimbell Art Museum in Texas, US, and the National Assembly Building in Dhaka, Bangladesh.

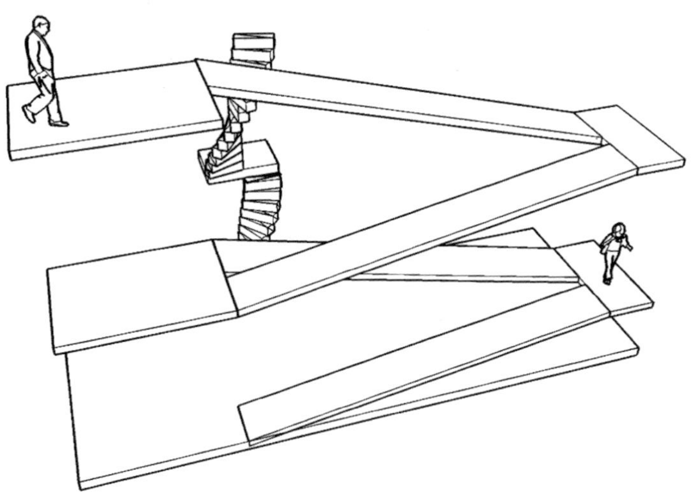

7. Plan of Villa Savoye
Le Corbusier celebrated the journey around and the route through the Villa Savoye, using ramps and stairs to connect the movement around the building with the views and vistas from it. Enfilade (taken from the French, meaning to thread or to pass through from end to end) refers to a suite of rooms with doorways that align with one another. The Villa Savoye is planned in this way so that the rooms too connect and open up to create a journey through the building.

8. Plan of the Château de Versailles
This plan of the Château de Versailles provides an example of enfilade planning; it incorporates a series of rooms that are connected together along an axis.

ROUTE

The route in a building is critical. The route to a building's door or entrance will be any visitor's first experience of the architecture. How this journey then continues through the building, the connections between the outside and the inside and the different interior levels, will further enhance the experience.

In some buildings, such as museums and galleries, this route may be designed as part of the architectural concept. The route through these buildings might allow, in this instance, the art or artifacts to be better understood and experienced. Buildings can also have strong relationships to the journeys or routes around them; a promenade, for example, celebrates the movement around a building or structure.

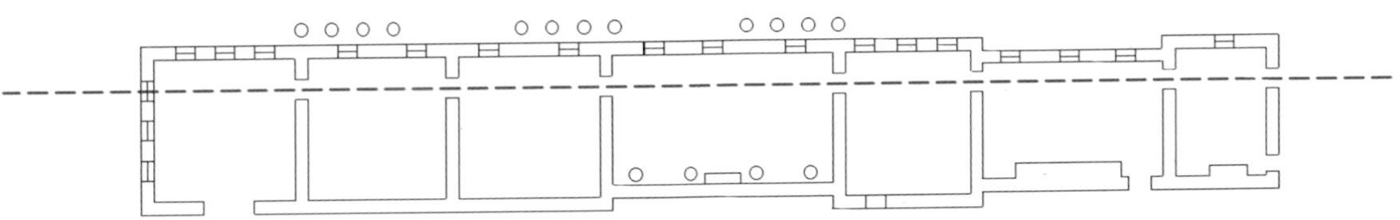

Functionalism

'Form follows function' was a phrase coined by American architect **Louis Sullivan**. It described a means of redirecting architecture and followed the premise that the form of any building should be defined by the activities that were to be carried out inside it, rather than any historical precedent or aesthetic ideal. Sullivan designed the world's first skyscrapers using these functionalist design principles.

The concept of functionalism was further developed by Austrian architect Adolf Loos. He wrote of 'ornament as crime', and was a proponent of the argument that any decoration on a building was both superfluous and unnecessary. The thinking of both architects created new and modern responses to architectural design.

MODERNISM

Modernism was a huge architectural influence in the twentieth century and, as its name suggests, the modernist movement embraced the moment. Modernism interacted with a dynamic that brought together political, social and cultural changes. Most expressive minimal and organic styles refer to modernism in some way.

Modernist architecture is a term given to a number of building styles with similar characteristics, primarily the simplification of form and the elimination of ornament, that first arose around 1900. The modernist architects responded to the concepts of 'form following function' and 'ornament as crime' and their architecture, adopting forms that derived from the response to the functions or activities within the buildings, and leaving the buildings devoid of any adornment, produced characteristically clean white spaces.

By the 1940s these styles had been consolidated and became the dominant architectural style for institutional and corporate building for several decades in the twentieth century.

9

10

9. Isokon Lawn Road Flats, London, UK
Wells Coates, 1934
These apartments were purposefully designed using the application of modernist principles. The architecture is bright, practical and very functional, and the furniture was also purpose-designed for the interior spaces. These apartments also incorporated some of the UK's first examples of fitted kitchens, which offered potential occupants a practical and contemporary lifestyle.

10. Villa Savoye (interior), Paris, France
Le Corbusier, 1928–1929
Le Corbusier's Villa Savoye introduced a new type of open-plan building. Its light interior spaces and the absence of any decoration or adornment presented a practical, simple and functional approach to living.

Louis Sullivan 1856–1924
An American architect, Sullivan is most notably associated with the design of the skyscraper, which became a real possibility when the development of steel-framed buildings and construction technology advanced (the Carson Pirie Scott department store in Chicago is Sullivan's most famous steel-framed building). His approach was concerned with form following function and the buildings he produced were driven by functional necessity.

11. The Farnsworth House, Illinois, US
Ludwig Mies van der Rohe, 1946–1950
The Farnsworth House is one of the more famous examples of modernist domestic architecture and was considered unprecedented in its day. Transcending any traditional domestic function, the importance of this house lies in the absolute purity and consistency of its architectural idea.

11

THE MODERNIST FOUNDERS

By the 1920s the most important figures in modern architecture had established their reputations. The three 'founders' are commonly recognised as Le Corbusier in France, and Ludwig Mies van der Rohe and Walter Gropius in Germany.

Mies van der Rohe and Gropius were both directors of the Bauhaus School (1919–1938), one of a number of European schools and associations concerned with reconciling craft tradition and industrial technology. The Bauhaus was one of the most influential schools of architecture, art and design of the twentieth century. Its pedagogy required a new approach, one that explored the functionality and practicality of design, housed workshops and studios, and taught architecture through aspects of contemporary culture, film, dance, art and product design. The Bauhaus promoted a new unity between art and technology, and encouraged thinking and designs that responded to both technology and ideology.

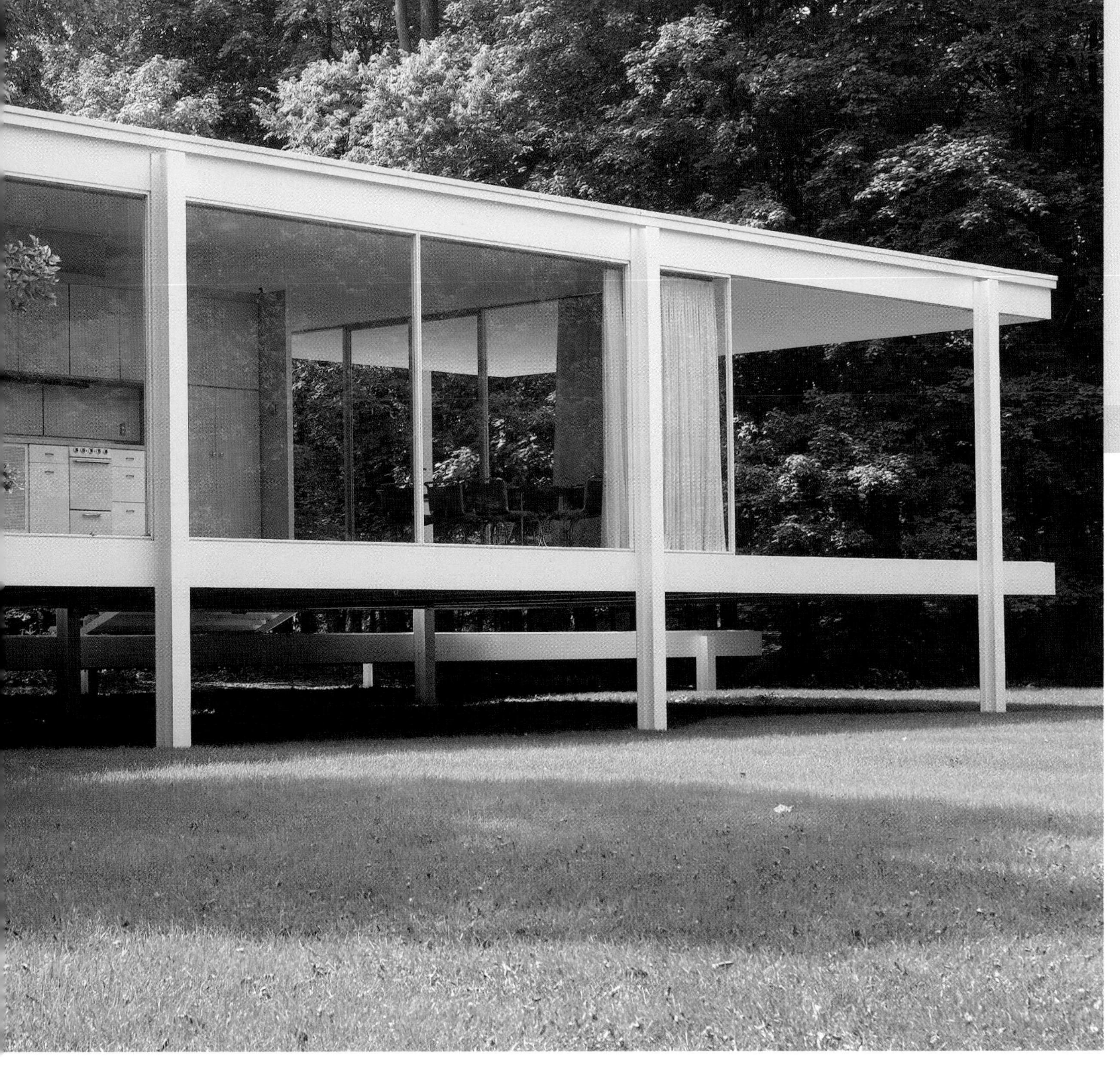

Sculpturalism

The modernist dogma, which saw the function of a building affect its final shape and form, was to produce a reactive and opposing school of architectural thought. Sculpturalism dictates that function follows form, that the shape of a building should be the architect's primary consideration, and any functions and activities that the building is to house should be accommodated into this form.

Organic architecture describes a design approach where the form is dominant and is influenced by fluid and dynamic shapes. The construction of this type of structural form can usually only be achieved using innovative materials and cutting-edge technology to assist with the design of the spaces and the manufacture of the building. One of the earliest architects who embraced the ideals of organic architecture was Antoni Gaudí; his most famous work, La Sagrada Familia, or the Parc Güel (both in Barcelona, Spain) use forms in a sculptural way to great dynamic effect.

Sculptural architecture is also exemplified by the work of Frank Gehry and his use of materials in groundbreaking and jaw-dropping ways. Gehry's architectural ideas are initially created and designed using a sculptural process too. Sculptural architecture works well with flexible materials and a fine example of this is Gehry's Guggenheim Museum in Bilbao, Spain. The museum uses heavy limestone blocks at the base, and titanium metal sheets, which curve and reflect light, form the walls and the roof. The combination of materials and the forms that they are made to adopt creates a striking contrast with the rectilinear forms of the city.

Both sculptural and organic design approaches require all the activities of a building to be fitted into the dramatic shape or form. In the best examples of this architecture, the interior and exterior experience work together to impressive effect.

12

12. La Sagrada Familia, Barcelona, Spain
Antoni Gaudí, still to be completed
La Sagrada Familia is extremely ornamental and decorative. It looks like it has been sculpted rather than built and its stones appear almost liquid-like and display a light, open quality. This challenges our preconceptions of a heavy stone structure.

13

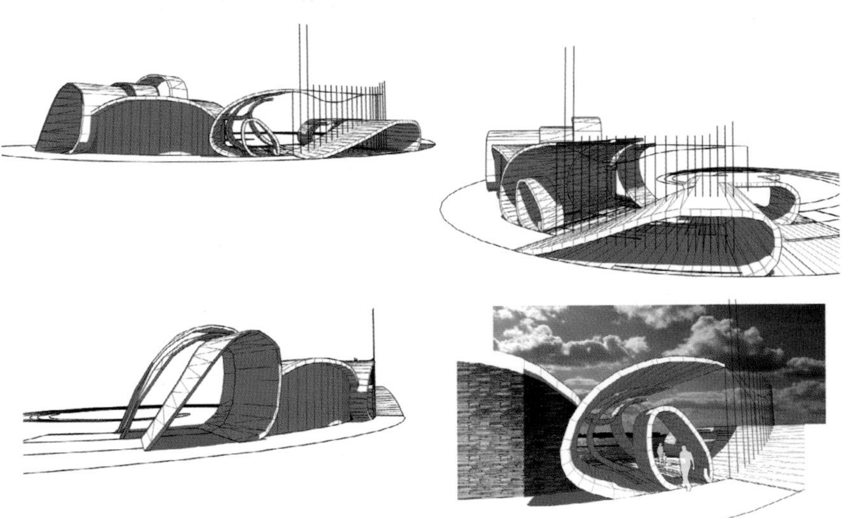

14

13. Frederick R. Weisman Art Museum, Minneapolis, US
Frank Gehry, 1993
This museum is a great example of function following form. Gehry's architecture uses the form primarily to determine the building; its materiality and shape are the main considerations.

14. Organic Form
Organic forms and shapes can be designed using physical and CAD modelling techniques. Doing so allows you to explore the potential of the idea and exploit forms in architecture.

15

SCULPTURAL INTERIORS

Buildings can have both dramatic exteriors and produce organic or sculptural forms, and also contain an interior experience that is equally dynamic. Floors, walls and ceilings can challenge convention and slope inward or outward to great theatrical effect. Sloped ceilings and floor planes working together can create an incredibly exaggerated effect, extending the sense of perspective inside a space. Equally, walls can be constructed to exaggerate the perceived height of a space. This creates an architectural illusion; our perception of these spaces is altered through careful use of material and form.

This type of building creates unexpected encounters, sloping floors and leaning walls, for example, produce a gravity-defying experience. In such a building everything needs to be reconsidered, from the lighting and furniture, to the apertures for walls and windows. The relationship from the outside to the inside of the architecture is particularly dramatic. New types of lightweight composite materials have made architecture of this sort a real possibility.

15. Phaeno Science Centre, Wolfsburg, Germany
Zaha Hadid, 2000–2005
This building challenges conventional and traditional shapes and forms and is typical of Zaha Hadid's ideas, which are both sculptural and dynamic. The Phaeno Science Centre is a new paradigm for architecture; dynamic shapes are formed as the building acts like a landscape, with the different levels of the exhibition space positioned at different heights within it. The spaces challenge most preconceived ideas about a building; it is almost impossible to determine where the walls stop and the floor or ceiling begins.

16. Educatorium Utrecht University, Utrecht, The Netherlands
OMA (Office for Metropolitan Architecture), 1997
This building was part of a masterplan for the university that was created by OMA. The educatorium has a concrete floor that appears to wrap around the building and become the roof too, questioning the idea of separate surfaces for roof, wall and floor.

Monumentalism

A building that is monumental has meaning beyond its form and function. It can be monumental both in its scale and in terms of what it represents. Monuments have been constructed to celebrate important events and people for centuries. Some of these structures still exist and are a part of our culture today; think perhaps of Stonehenge or the pyramids at Giza. Buildings that become synonymous with more than their function, perhaps with a city or a culture, could be described as monumental.

DUAL PURPOSE

Some buildings have become synonymous with their location and the identity of it. If one considers any major city it's possible to think of a building or structure associated with it, the White House in Washington, Buckingham Palace in London or the Musée du Louvre in Paris, for example. All these buildings have meaning associated with them beyond their architecture. They have become icons of their location.

There is another, more contemporary, idea of a building or space that works as a monument and also celebrates an important event or is a place for cultural events to take place (and/or has a cultural or national significance). Examples of these include Times Square, the Sydney Opera House, the Eiffel Tower and Trafalgar Square. Such buildings or spaces can be described as having a dual purpose

17. La Bibliothèque Nationale, Paris, France
Dominique Perrault, 1989–1997
La Bibliothèque Nationale, know affectionately to Parisians as 'TGB' (Trés Grande Bibliothèque) challenges our understanding of library spaces and how they interact with the city. The building is accessed by climbing a series of steps onto a platform that looks across the River Seine. One then descends along an inclined travelator into the library.

Once inside there is an internalised open garden, which has trees of quite an unexpected scale. In this building the books and resources are almost secondary to the experience of arrival and movement into the building. It is of an enormous scale and a series of book 'towers ' identify the TGB unmistakably on the Parisian skyline.

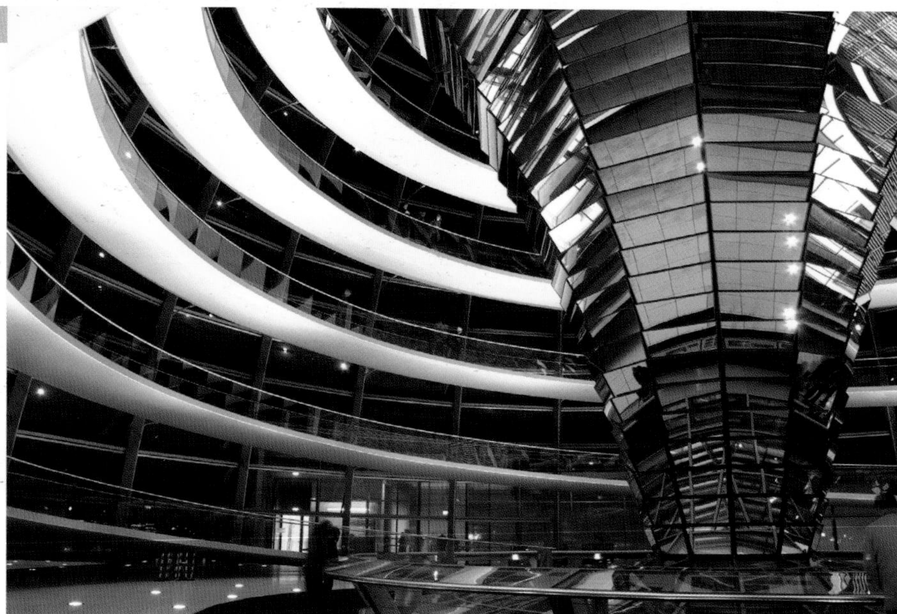

18. The Reichstag (interior), Berlin, Germany Foster + Partners, 1992–1999
Built originally in 1894, the Reichstag was damaged by fire in 1933. A glass dome and complete interior renovation project was completed in 1999. The dome is intended to represent a transparent democracy for the German people.

PARLIAMENT BUILDINGS

Parliament buildings also fall into the category of monumental architecture as they have a national symbolism and often connect with a cultural identity. A new parliament building needs to represent a nation in terms of its architectural form, its materiality and its presence.

The German parliament building, the Reichstag, uses materials that reinforce architectural and political metaphors. This nineteenth-century building was redesigned and reinterpreted by Foster + Partners in 1999 and its architecture is underpinned by a transparent structure, which is intended to reflect the ideal of a transparent, open and modern democracy in government.

The glass-domed structure has a ramp within it, so one can look down from above into the debating chamber, to watch the activity of parliament. The Reichstag building was a symbol of reunification and the reinvention of modern Germany.

Spanish architect Enric Miralles, working in conjunction with RMJM architects, designed the Scottish Parliament building in 2004. This building could be described as an example of function following form.

The construction of the parliament building was indicative of the start of a new political era in Scotland, and the building's architecture was intended to reinforce Scottish identity and culture. The building has many references and metaphors from nature and uses a palette of local materials including stones, granites and oak, which have been interpreted in a contemporary way to create dramatic and unexpected shapes and forms.

The Welsh Assembly building by Richard Rogers Partnership is again an example of a new parliament for a new political era. The building is subtle, appearing as a light, pavilion-like structure covered in glass, framing views across Cardiff bay and the emerging commercial development. It uses materials simply and lightly and has a strong connection with its surrounding outside space.

21

20

19. & 20. Welsh Assembly Building (interior detail and exterior), Cardiff, UK
Richard Rogers Partnership, 1998–2005
This building opens out to views across Cardiff bay and is a light open structure that sits easily on its site.

The ceiling of the Welsh Assembly Building reflects the forms of a sandy beach, as this detail shows.

21. Scottish Parliament, Edinburgh, UK
Enric Miralles, 1998–2004
The new Scottish parliament building in Edinburgh represents a new future for Scotland. This is celebrated with a bold building where function follows form. It uses many local materials to create a dynamic exterior form and unexpected interior spaces.

Zeitgeist

The German term zeitgeist refers to the spirit of a time. In terms of design this is an inevitably changing and shifting notion. The zeitgeist naturally evolves as it responds to current social and cultural phenomena.

At the beginning of the twentieth century, design was responding to modernist ideals and approaches. The modernist style and its use of materials and form originated in Europe and, although not applicable in all contexts, had enormous influence in other regions across the world. The concept of an 'international' style was based on the notion that a style or design could exist across many cultures and have no boundaries.

One of the strengths of the international style was that the design solutions were indifferent to location, site, and climate. This was one of the reasons it was called 'international'; the style made no reference to local history or national vernacular. Later this was identified as one of the style's primary weaknesses.

The modernist style has, however, been adapted by some to accommodate local conditions. Examples of this are Oscar Niemeyer's architecture in Brazil and Luis Barragan's work in Mexico. Their style is modern in form, but uses bolder form and colour as it is influenced by local traditions.

22

23

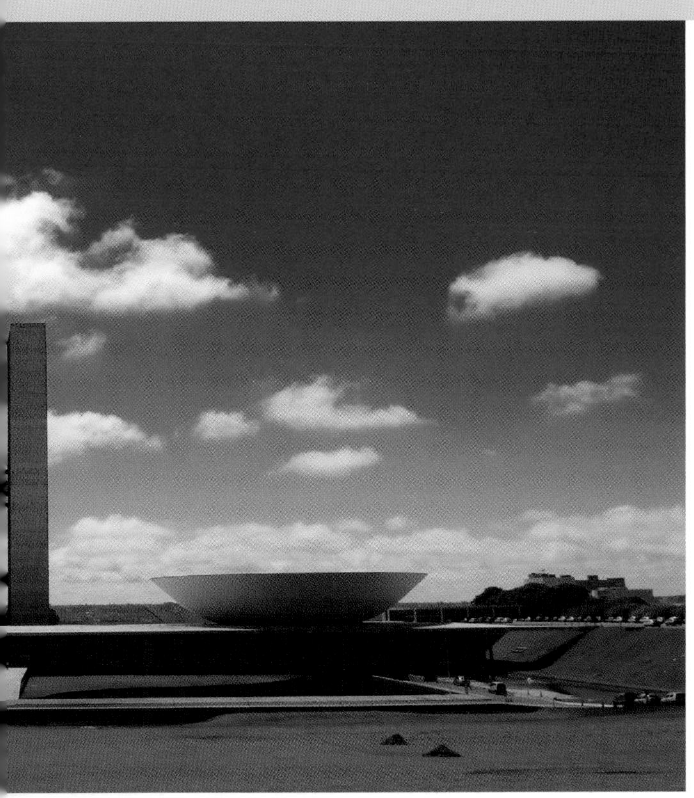

22. The National Congress, Brasilia, Brazil
Oscar Niemeyer, 1958–1960
Niemeyer organised a competition for the urbanistic layout of Brasilia and the winner was the proposal of his old master and friend, Lúcio Costa. Niemeyer would design the buildings and Lúcio the plan of the city.

Taking his lead from modernist ideals, Niemeyer designed a large number of residential, commercial and government buildings. Among them were the residence of the President, the House of the Deputy, the National Congress, as well as many residential buildings. Viewed from above, the city can be seen to have elements that repeat themselves in every building, giving it a formal unity.

23. Munich Airport Centre (MAC), Munich, Germany
Murphy Jahn Architects, 1989–1999
The Munich Airport Centre defines the airport in an era of globalisation. It is a place in itself, a destination that integrates transportation, commerce, technology and landscape. There is a relationship between travel, work, shopping and entertainment that allows the airport to become a complete architectural experience.

24. The Barcelona Pavilion (interior)
Ludwig Mies van der Rohe, 1928–1929
This is an interior detail of a marble wall inside the Barcelona Pavilion. The pavilion was built from glass, travertine and different kinds of marble.

25. Museum of Contemporary Art Barcelona, Barcelona, Spain
Richard Meier, 1994–1996
Meier has a consistent approach and style to his architecture. The cool, white light qualities and distinct areas of shadow in the spaces create interest. He has designed many galleries that are distinctive and provide a white neutral background against which to read the artworks.

25

MATERIALS

To understand the possibilities and limitations of materials is an important aspect of architecture. Whether it be an understanding of both contemporary and historical uses of a material or the testing of an innovative approach to its application or use, this knowledge informs and underpins the design process.

The material quality of a building has to relate to its site and environment (the exterior), and to its function and users (the interior). These are very different requirements, but the specification of the materials must reconcile the interior and exterior demands of the building. To learn how to develop this skill it is important for architects to see how materials need to sit together, are fixed together and how they can coexist and complement one another.

24

STYLE

Style represents a response to culture and can be viewed as a kind of fashion or popular trend. In architecture, as in many other cultural art forms, very often these styles are referred to as 'isms'. Classicism is a style informed by classical architecture and culture. Similarly, modernism was influenced by modern culture of the 1920s and 1930s.

Labels that attach themselves to these styles are varied. Some are very particular while others are much looser. It is important to appreciate the affect that each 'ism' has had on succeeding styles and to remember that all design comes from an understanding of precedent, whether historic, cultural or social. The invention and originality of design comes from its application and timing in contemporary culture: its appropriateness for now.

The question of style is a difficult issue for architecture generally, as it has aesthetic as well as functional parameters. If architecture is too attached to contemporary style it will quickly appear 'unfashionable', which is problematic as architecture needs to be durable. The most enduring architectural concepts and ideas have accommodated changing cultures, users and functions.

Chapter 6
Realisation

This chapter explores an architectural project from inception through to completion, showing the stages through which an architectural project is realised.

This process is a type of journey; there is a narrative or story attached to the making of a building, from its initial concept to the finished construction. Following a project through each of these stages will demonstrate that a diverse range of skills, from conceptual thinking to practical construction, are involved. This chapter looks at each of these stages in terms of a 'real' project.

1

1. Architect's Impression
This perspective CAD image shows Design Engine Architects' impression of their proposal for the new British Embassy building in Sana'a, Yemen.

1. Concept (page 156)

i

i. Concept Sketch

2. Site Analysis (page 158)

ii

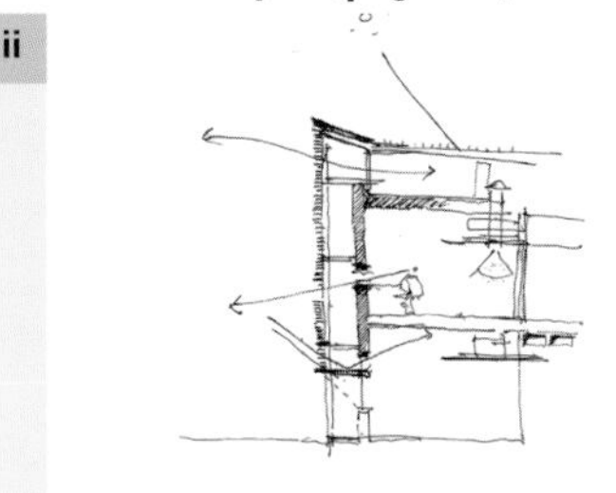

iii

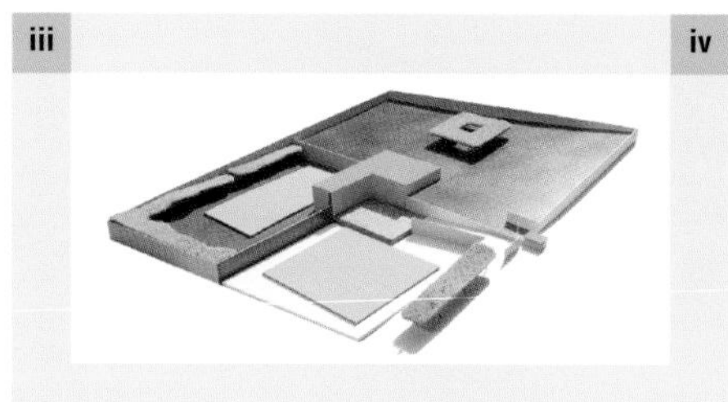

iv

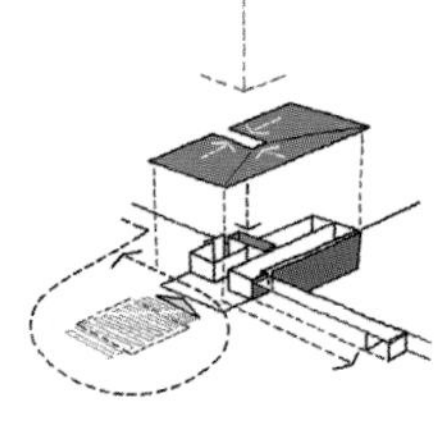

3. Design Process (page 160)

v

vi

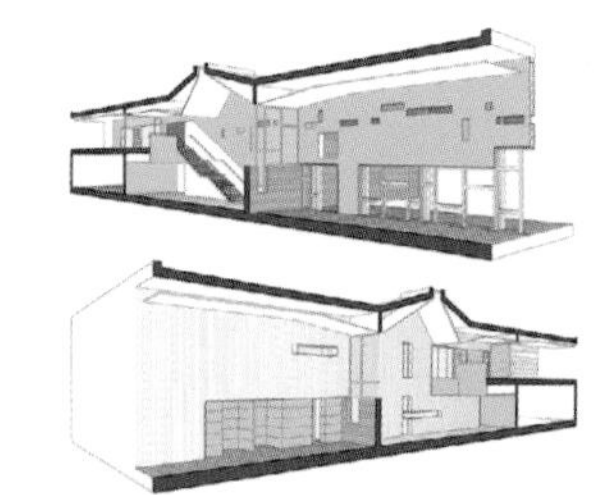

vii

4. Detail Development (page 162)

ix

x

ix. On Site

x. Construction Takes Shape

5. The Finished Building (page 164)

xi

xii

xiii

The Project Timeline

Depending on time and complexity, projects vary in time, but in each case their realisation represents a journey that tells the story of how a building is made. This timeline shows the five key stages of a project's realisation: concept, site analysis, the design process, construction and detail development and the result. Each of the sections identified in the timeline will be described in more detail later in the chapter.

ii. Sectional Sketch

iii. Concept Model

iv. Three-dimensional Sketch

viii

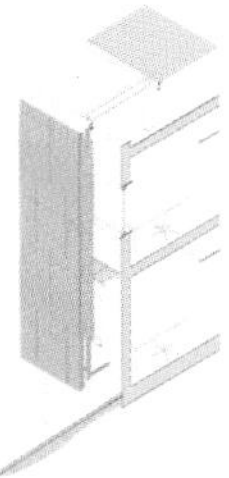

v. Perspective-rendered Drawing

vi. Section Drawing

vii. Perspective Sketch

viii. Detail Drawing

xiv

xi. The Finished Building

xii & xiii The Building's Wrapping

xiv. Dynamic Surfaces

The Project

The project is the realisation of the British Embassy Building in Sana'a, Yemen, which was completed in 2006. The commission was won in an international competition set by the British Foreign Office in 2003. A British practice, Design Engine Architects, won the commission, responding directly to the brief of producing a proposal for 'a flagship building that demonstrates the best of British architecture'.

The embassy building is situated within a challenging site, and has to contend with desert-like conditions, where temperatures can be very hot in the day and very cold at night, and Design Engine also found there were challenges to the nature of the brief as well as the site. The building needed to provide a secure, yet accessible service to the local community and create a representative cultural interface for Great Britain. These issues informed the organisation of the building's internal layout, the choice of materials used and the relationships between outside gardens and inside rooms.

2. The roof of the building overhangs the wall of the embassy, protecting it from the overhead sun. As the sun moves across the building the moving shadow animates the exterior elevations.

3. The glazed wall frames views across the landscape and allows light to filter into the inside spaces. Shadows move slowly across the wall and floors, defining interior features and details.

2

3

Contributors and Their Roles

The realisation of any project will involve a vast team of people, and each member of that team will have different skills that can be applied at different stages of the design and construction processes. Central to the success of any architectural project will be ensuring that the team works well together and that the necessary project information is communicated clearly among all members of the team.

THE CLIENT

The client initiates the project, provides the funds for construction and is usually the building's end user. The best clients will have aspirations for their building, and these will be translated clearly into a range of activities and functionality that they want the architecture to accommodate. For example, they may have a vision in terms of what internal and external environments they expect the building to provide them with, or have expectations about what the building needs to symbolise or represent.

All these requirements, desires and functions will then be shaped into a project brief, which is used by the architect as a springboard and measure of their design ideas.

SURVEYORS

Surveyors measure different aspects of building. A **building surveyor** measures the material and fabric of the architecture and produces drawings of an existing building on site or the location and levels of extant site features. The information in these drawings allows the site parameters to be better understood before the architect begins to consider the building's design. For example, if the site is sloped this will affect what it is possible to build.

Building surveyors can also be involved in establishing boundaries of sites and buildings. Specialists such as historic building surveyors have specific knowledge of older buildings, which can also be valuable.

A **quantity surveyor** measures the building's materials and by itemising and costing all these, provides an estimate of the project costs. Together with the brief and survey drawings, these projections are used to form the contract or instructions that will indicate how the building is to be constructed.

ENGINEERS

Engineers are concerned with the technical application of scientific understanding to design. In short, they design systems in conjunction with the architect, whether it be the building's structure or its heating, ventilation or electrical solutions.

Structural engineers work with the various aspects of a building's structure, including the frame, the foundations and the façades. They advise, inform and design structural aspects of the building, from its overall frame through to individual details such as the size of structural supports or fixings. A structural engineer will demonstrate the viability of the building and rationalise its structural elements so that they are efficient, effective and complement the overall architectural idea.

A **mechanical engineer** is, broadly, someone who is involved with the design, development and installation of machinery. In building terms this refers to the designer of the building's mechanical, heating and ventilation systems. These systems need to be considered, specific and integrated into the design idea so that they work effectively with the spatial material and formal architectural concepts.

Electrical engineers work very closely with the mechanical engineers to design and oversee the installation of the electrical systems for the building. On larger projects, electrical engineers can work with lighting consultants to provide a specific lighting strategy for the building.

Acoustic engineers deal with aspects of noise control. They understand how sounds move through the building's materials, and can suggest specifications that will affect the user's experience of sound in the building. When buildings need to accommodate many and varied functions, acoustic engineers can advise about separation of structures, such as walls or floors, to reduce sound transmission. Additionally they can advise on material specifications that can alter sound appreciation in space.

LANDSCAPE ARCHITECTS

All architecture is positioned in a location or context; landscape architects are concerned with connecting a building to its surroundings.

Landscape architects will start by analysing the site to understand specific climatic condition, such as rainfall, amount of sunlight or temperature range, and to understand the area's indigenous plants and their planting conditions.

Landscape design also considers aspects of the journey and route through the building's external spaces, and the activities associated with those spaces. Good landscape design binds a building into its site, complements all aspects of the architecture and is inseparable from the building.

CONTRACTORS

Building contractors physically construct the building, working with information provided by engineers, architects and surveyors. Generally they are directed by a project manager or architect on site. Some projects may also obtain the services of subcontractors or specialists to make something in a particular way or using a special technique.

Building contractors adhere to a schedule of works that they devise at the start of the project to ensure that the materials, tradesmen and services are all coordinated to allow the building project to progress smoothly. The integration of these different services is critical to the successful completion of the building.

The Brief

The brief is written to limit and define the project specifications, determining aspects of function, construction, materiality and relationship to site. The brief is composed initially as a response to the client's intentions for the site, and is then further developed to provide detailed information about the project requirements, including, among other factors, appraisal of site, accommodation requirements, internal layout requirements and specialised fittings and fixtures.

Yemen, at the southern end of the Arabian Peninsula, is a fascinating country with a hospitable people and a wealth of cultural heritage, landscape and architectural tradition. The existing British Embassy in Sana'a (the capital) had become a dispiriting place to work. It occupied a pair of Ottoman-era villas on a city-centre plot, each of which was almost buried by a mound of vast protective sandbags. By 2003 it was obvious that if Britain was to maintain a diplomatic presence in Yemen then a new building would be urgently required.

For several years the British Foreign and Commonwealth Office (FCO) has adopted a policy of using design competitions to select architects for their new building commissions. The FCO kept faith with this strategy for the new building in Yemen, and in August 2003 the competition was won by Design Engine Architects, working in conjunction with Whitbybird engineers.

The FCO introduced Design Engine to the paradoxical nature of their brief by explaining that 'on the one hand the ideal Embassy is a highly secure underground bunker, however on the other hand it needs to be a marquee on a lawn with a large sign saying "do come in and have a cup of tea"'.

At the outset of the design process, with 9/11 and the bombing of the British Embassy in Istanbul fresh in the mind, Design Engine sometimes felt that it was an indulgence to be concerned with issues of architectural composition, materiality and landscape. It forced them to ask why not choose to follow the American 'off-the-shelf' style of embassy design. These buildings bore little relation to their context, but were proven to be highly functional and secure. But Design Engine felt that for the FCO, an embassy building needs to be a visual expression of their diplomatic approach, one based upon engagement and partnership rather than the exercise of overwhelming power. As such, an 'off-the-shelf' fortress would not be appropriate.

4

5

6

4. An interior CAD impression of the embassy's reception area.

5. An interior CAD impression the embassy's office spaces.

6. An interior CAD impression of the embassy's circulation spaces.

7

8

7. An interior CAD impression of the embassy's double-height reception area.

8. An interior CAD impression of one of the embassy's informal public access spaces.

The Concept

The concept is the driving idea of the project and it will respond to the architecture's function, site and brief, as well as any historic or typological precedents.

Developing the concept from sketch to a fully functional building, one which refers back to and connects with the initial ideas, is a challenge. Because of this, concepts for architectural projects need to be clear and understood by all members of the team so that they can inform and be reinforced at all stages of the project's development.

THE PROJECT CONCEPT

The concept for Design Engine's embassy building was to reveal and celebrate two pivotal aspects of the project brief: the idea of a solid protected box and that of an open elegant marquee.

Design Engine saw it as their job to reconcile this central paradox. It was not a question of either/or, in this case the building was to be both bunker and marquee. Their objective was to create a highly secure building, which was also generous and respectful towards its context in the host country.

Design Engine's approach was to reveal and celebrate this duality, rather than to hide it. Their concept for the body of the building was an honestly expressed boardmark-finished concrete box, which would be bedded into the sloping site. This form would be eroded at the northeast corner, creating a public face and a sense of openness, and, where the perimeter wall gives way to railings, also allowing the public a view of the building across a formal 'lawn'.

The elevations of the 'concrete box' were to be veiled by a brise soleil made from Corten weathering steel. This screen would then serve both as a means of providing shade and as a sacrificial outer layer of the building.

Corten is a robust material that is often used in civil engineering structures due to the fact that once the protective oxide layer is established it requires virtually no maintenance. In this project Corten was to be used in a completely new way, achieving a surprisingly delicate appearance almost like an Islamic mashrabiya screen.

The roof of the building was also to be screened with a steel canopy, which would create a strong horizontal datum on the sloping site.

9

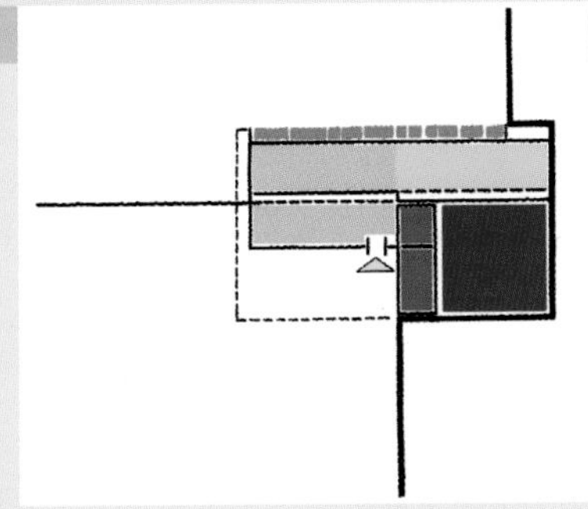

10

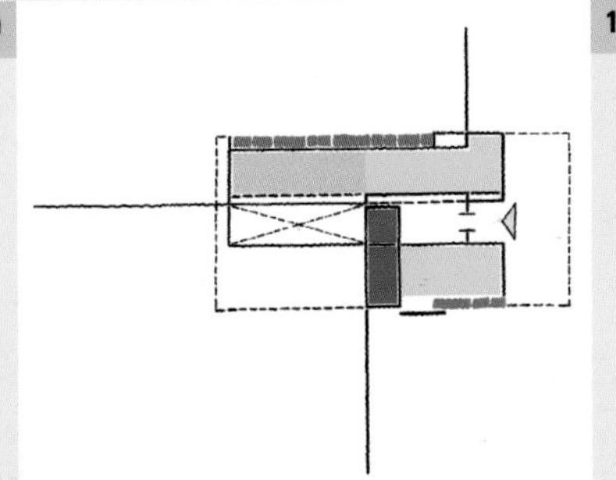

11

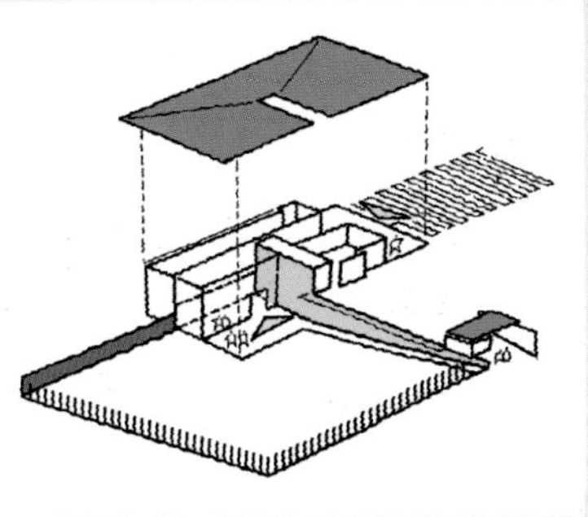

12

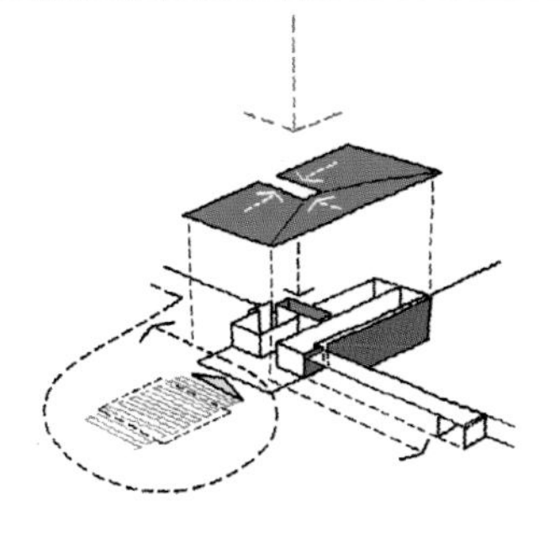

9. This concept sketch outlines the way in which the embassy's main public entrance connects to the outside lawn.

10. A concept sketch showing a more private staff entrance.

11. A concept sketch providing a view of the embassy's large, all-enclosing roof.

12. This concept sketch shows varying arrival and circulation points in the embassy.

13. A sketch of the embassy's main entrance area.

13

Site Analysis

Site analysis is a process that allows for specific aspects of the project's location to inform the design idea. For example, there may be historical precedents, say in terms of building design or construction techniques, which are particular to that locality, or climate ranges and average temperatures that may affect the relationship between a building's interior and exterior. All these factors, and more, can affect the design ideas.

Analysing and understanding the immediate locality and the surrounding area will allow the design to better connect with both the site and its context.

THE PROJECT SITE ANALYSIS

The site of the embassy building sits at the foot of Jabal Nugum, one of several peaks that surround Sana'a. To the north the city dissolves into rocky desert in a sprawl of warehouses and half-completed buildings. Below and to the west are the minarets of Old Sana'a. In the evening, as the setting sun turns the mountainside red and the sound of the muezzin drifts up from the old town, the site has a sense of tranquillity and a raw, tough beauty. In this environment, the earthy combination of Corten steel and boardmarked concrete seems to fit perfectly.

In this project the slope of the site was a key informer of design. The landscape strategy for dealing with the sloping site was to create a series of terraces that would help to unobtrusively segregate the different users of the building as they move around the external spaces. These landscape terraces create artificial horizons that exclude the foreground clutter from view while having the surprising effect of seeming to bring the mountainside closer, giving it great presence within the site.

14. This model shows the scheme as a series of walled gardens, allowing the building to relate to the landscape while remaining a secure environment.

15. There are many aspects of local architectural features that influenced the development of the design idea. These houses appear to have solid walls from the outside, yet on the inside light filters through geometric patterns of stained glass. This was an idea that influenced the design of the glazing in the embassy.

14

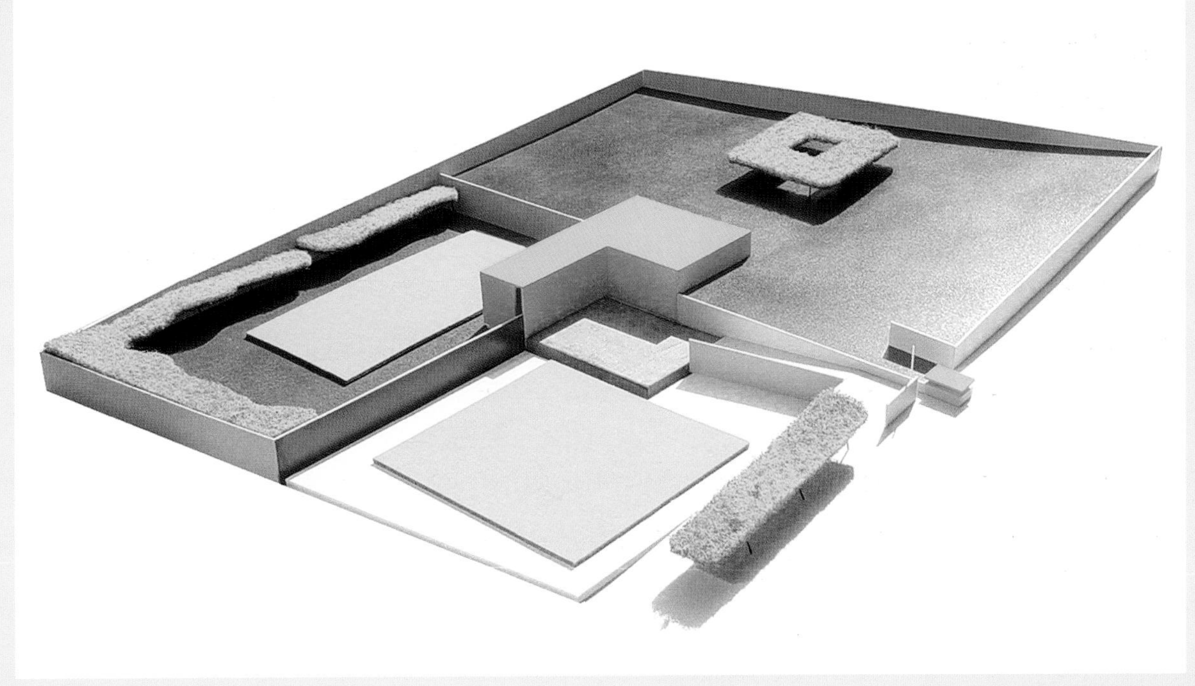

15

The Design Process

The process of designing a building is an unpredictable journey. It starts as a concept, perhaps represented as a series of sketches or some models, but as the idea develops, key considerations and decisions have to be made by the client. These will concern the use of individual spaces, the functional requirements of the building and its surroundings, the use of materials, or the heating, ventilation and lighting strategies. The decisions taken on all of these sort of issues should reinforce the initial architectural concept. During the design process it is vital that the key concept is retained and that any decision-making does not compromise the integrity of the idea.

PROJECT DESIGN PROCESS

In keeping with the aim of creating an inclusive building, the project design attempts to bring together British technology with Yemen's rich architectural, landscape and construction traditions.

Design Engine was assisted by an experienced local conservation architect who helped provide the specifications for the building's stone and mud walls and identified craftsmen who were capable of carrying out work to an exemplary standard.

The building's major walls, which extend into the landscape, are constructed from Habash, a porous volcanic stone used widely in Sana'a's many historical buildings. The face of each Habash stone was hand chiselled and laid using a technique referred to as 'mohanash'. Employing this technique meant that each finished face inclined outward slightly, so that at the top of each course there was a step of 3–5 mm. This subtle construction detail means that as the sun moves overhead the wall is suddenly transformed, with the courses appearing in bright relief.

The building's mud walls were built using a technique particular to Sana'a. The best mud was recycled from collapsed buildings and mixed with sharp stones and straw to help bind it together. This was then laid in courses that were 500mm deep by 500mm wide, and each layer was reinforced with sticks and branches.

The Yemen's local tradition of coloured glass as a building material found contemporary expression in the embassy building via a series of slot windows that animated the Corten upper façade at the building's north-east corner. The inner face of this façade was clad in oak panelling, and this language of wood and glass continued through the spine of the building providing a visual link and an illusion of connectivity across three spaces that are in fact strictly separated.

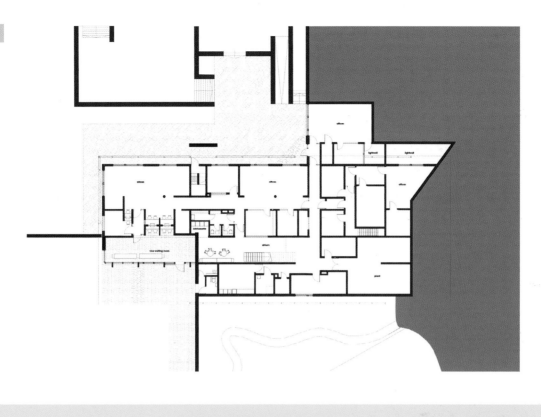

16

16. A layout plan of the embassy indicating the relationship to its garden spaces.

17. These section drawings show the relationships across the spaces inside the scheme.

17

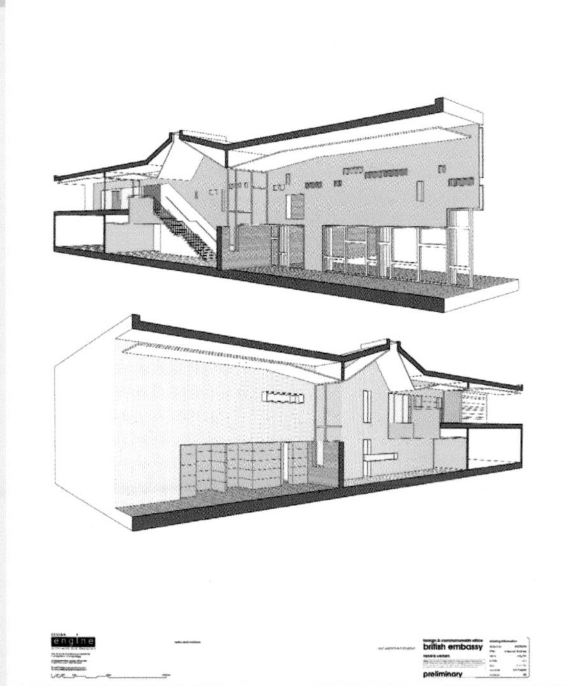

Detail Development

At this stage in the project, drawings are produced to allow the building to be constructed. These drawings will vary in scale and number; bespoke elements will need lots of detail to explain construction whereas other, more standard, aspects of construction will need little detailed explanation or drawings.

PROJECT DETAIL DEVELOPMENT

The intensity of the sun in the Yemen required detailed consideration of the building's windows and apertures in order to ensure that the temperature range inside the embassy remained at comfortable levels. Design Engine developed a bespoke system to modify the light coming into the building in the form of a brise soleil, which reduced the amount of direct sunlight entering the building, thus preventing the internal temperature from increasing.

The screen idea was developed from an initial sketch. This sketch was further developed in the form of a section drawing, which allowed Design Engine to consider aspects of scale and the effect of the different angle of the sun at different times of the day. The concept was further investigated using a detailed CAD model. The CAD modelling allowed light to be predicted both at different times of the day and at various points in the year to fully test the design concept. The screen needed to be robust, as it was a protective layer, but equally as thin as possible so it did not appear as a solid wall. The modelling allowed the detail of the screen to evolve and develop until both requirements were satisfied.

A slightly unusual consideration for this project was that all aspects of the building's outer wall needed to be ultra secure. Therefore any glazing installed had to respond to the same security considerations. The glass used was designed, developed and manufactured specifically so that it could withstand bomb blasts. Making the glass bombproof required it to be laminated (or layered), which in turn made it extremely heavy. Because of its weight, the glass also had to incorporate a special detail so that it could be fixed to the frame securely; a standard window frame would have not provided sufficient support for the glass.

The design approach to these two details typifies the overall approach to the entire scheme. Most elements of the architecture were specially designed for this project. Despite their robustness, these bespoke details are subtle and they have been incorporated into a cohesive whole and complement one another very effectively. This is how the building succeeds as both a secure and yet open piece of architecture.

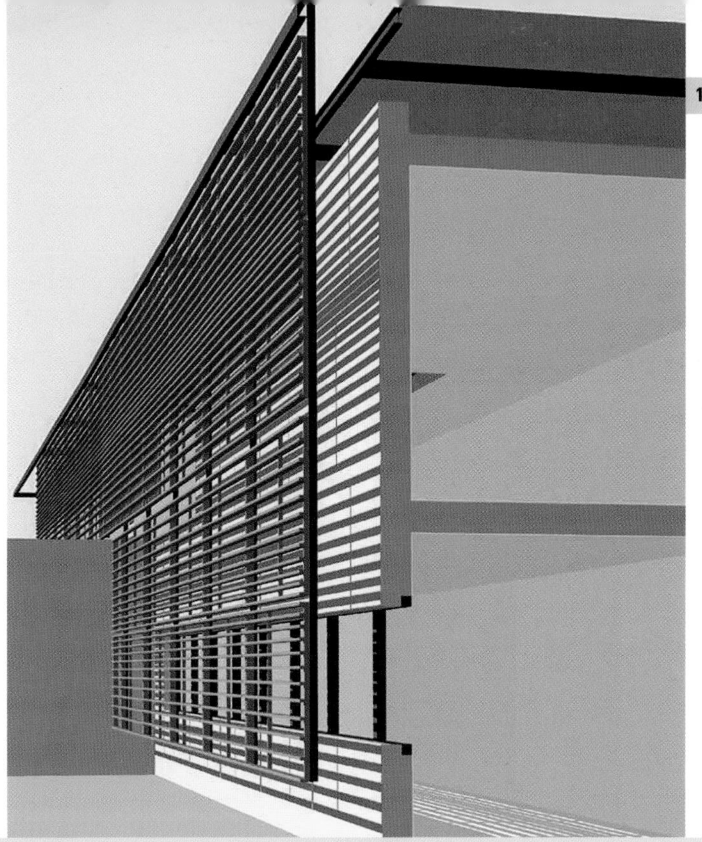

18. The embassy's brise soleil acts like a veil, moderating sunlight entering into the building and protecting the walls and glazing. This computer model predicts the light conditions on site.

19. & 20. The embassy's windows had to be designed to withstand bomb blasts. The windows were tested before installation to check that this requirement was satisfied.

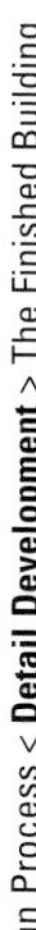

The Finished Building

All architecture needs to be imagined by the architect at the start of the project. The interesting aspect of any project is how well this imagined idea connects with the realised building. There are always aspects of architecture that surprise; even with complex physical and CAD models it is not always possible to predict, for example, the sensation of natural light changing the mood in a space. The experience of the interior spaces and how they connect cannot fully be understood until the building is finished. Once completed the success of any piece of architecture will reside on two key factors: does the building suit its intended purpose, and does it respond well to the initial brief?

THE FINISHED EMBASSY

The finished building embraces the central paradox of the brief: it is at once inviting and yet secure. Design Engine explored their idea in terms of its materiality and its relationship to landscape.

In material terms, the choice of concrete and steel is heavy and industrial. However they have been used with delicacy and care. Because of the way the concrete was treated (it was marked with timber), it appears softer, and the Corten steel screen has a terracotta colour, which connects it more to the softness of the ground than the hardness of its material properties.

The external screen covers the glazed areas of the building and this serves to mediate the exterior and the interior of the building. It protects the building from the surrounding high temperatures, but also acts as a light filter. This decision started off as a practical means to resolve issues of security and climate control, but has evolved to become a distinguishing feature of the building.

The screen has an ambiguity about it. When viewed from an angle it appears to be a solid wall or plane. However, when viewed from within the building, it appears light and the steel planes are reduced to thin lines. This summarises the effect of the building. It is a solid, heavily protected and secure box; however it is also a mediator between the local community and culture and the more distant British culture.

The relationship of the building to its external landscape is an aspect of the scheme that has worked particularly well. The architecture has an exterior hardness, but an interior softness. The way the building relates to its formal 'lawn', which serves as a kind of oasis in a hot inhospitable environment, is both unexpected and reassuring.

21

22

23

21. The finished building, with its low horizontal roof, relates clearly to the surrounding landscape.

22. The embassy's gardens soften its relationship to the landscape.

23. The Corten screen acts like a veil to protect the building, but yet it appears almost transparent at certain angles to allow views to the outside.

Conclusion

This book was designed to introduce the many and varied aspects of architecture and to simplify the complexity of the discipline. In so doing I hope to have inspired a creative curiosity and answered the questions of where architectural ideas and buildings come from and how are they made. The final chapter, realisation, shows the excitement and enormity of making architecture happen, and the journey's variables and possibilities.

I hope that this book has provided a window into the world of thinking, designing and making buildings, given you some tools to help you better see the architecture and the spaces around you, and provided you with an understanding of how to engage with buildings as architecture. The passion for architecture comes from our own child-like curiosity: the more we know about buildings, the more we realise we need to know. Keep looking for the clues of how and where the architectural ideas have come from; solving these clues is just like the excitement of revealing the present beneath the gift wrapping!

1

1. Flower Towers
David Mathias, 2002
This image brings together a range of architectural thinking and expression. It has been created using computer modelling and freehand drawing, and includes a plan, a perspective drawing and a strip elevation across an urban site.

Bibliography

Adler, D. (1999)
Metric Handbook Planning and Design Data (Second Edition)
The Architectural Press

Baker, G. (1996)
Design Strategies in Architecture: An Approach to the Analysis of Form
Von Nostrand Reinhold

Ching, F. (1995)
Architecture, Space, Form and Order
Von Nostrand Reinhold

Ching, F. (2002)
Architectural Graphics
John Wiley & Sons

Clark, R. and Pause, M. (1996)
Precedents in Architecture
John Wiley & Sons

Crowe, N. and Laseau, P. (1984)
Visual Notes for Architects and Designers
John Wiley & Sons

Curtis, W. (1996)
Modern Architecture Since 1900
Phaidon

Cullen, G. (1994)
Concise Landscape
The Architectural Press

Deplazes, A. (2005)
Constructing Architecture
Birkhauser

Fawcett, P. (2003)
Architecture Design Notebook
The Architectural Press

Le Corbusier (1986)
Towards a New Architecture
Architectural Press

Marjanovic, I. and Ray, K.R. (2003)
The Portfolio: An Architectural Press Student's Handbook
The Architectural Press

Porter, T. (2004)
Archispeak
Routledge

Porter, T. (1999)
Selling Architectural Ideas
Spon Press

Rasmussen, S. (1962)
Experiencing Architecture
M.I.T. Press

Richardson, P. (2001)
Big Ideas, Small Buildings
Thames & Hudson

Robbins, E. (1994)
Why Architects Draw
M.I.T. Press

Sharp, D. (1991)
The Illustrated Dictionary of Architects and Architecture
Headline Book Publishing

Unwin, S. (1997)
Analysing Architecture
Routledge

von Meiss, P. (1990)
Elements of Architecture
E & FN Spon Press

Weston, R. (2004)
Plans, Sections and Elevations
Laurence King Publishing

Weston, R. (2004)
Materials, Form and Architecture
Laurence King Publishing

Webography

archINFORM
www.archinform.net
This database for international architecture, originally emerging from records of interesting building projects from architecture students, has become the largest online database about worldwide architects and buildings from past to present.

Architecture Link
www.architecturelink.org.uk/homepage.html
Architecture Link aims to be the first port of call for all those interested in the subject of architecture and design. Its main objective is to foster public appreciation of architecture and the built environment, and also to provide a means for easily disseminating information on architecture and design.

From Here to Modernity
www.open2.net/modernity
Part of the BBC's Open University resource, this site tells the story of the modern movement in architecture through excellent narratives, video summaries and interviews, as well as a number of profiles of iconic buildings and prominent architects of the period.

Getty Images
www.gettyimages.com
This site makes available many images and visuals that can complement architectural presentation ideas.

Google Earth
www.earth.google.com
Google Earth combines satellite imagery and maps to make available the world's geographic information. Maps can be accessed to provide specific information about any site in the world at varying scales.

Great Buildings
www.greatbuildings.com
This is an architecture reference site that provides three-dimensional models, plans and photographic images of hundreds of international architects and their work.

International Union of Architects
www.uia-architects.org
The UIA is an international non-governmental organisation founded in Lausanne in 1948 to unite architects from all nations throughout the world, regardless of nationality, race, religion or architectural school of thought. The UIA is a unique world network uniting all architects.

Perspectives
www.archfilms.com
A Chicago-based resource, Perspectives produces high-quality videos on architecture and design. It also creates specialised videos and products for tourism planning, development firms, historic preservation agencies, cultural institutions and communities.

Royal Institute of British Architects (RIBA)
www.architecture.com
The RIBA website provides reference information and advice about the practice and training of architects.

SketchUp
www.sketchup.com
SketchUp is a piece of software that quickly creates a three-dimensional model of a building. It is an easy to use, intuitive program that produces models that look like they have been just been sketched freehand.

The American Institute of Architects
www.aia.org
This website has information about the education and practice of architecture in the USA.

Glossary

Acontextual
Buildings or ideas that deliberately react against their location in terms of material and/or form can be described as acontextual.

Anthropomorphic
Refers to the application of human characteristics or ideas to animals, natural elements and inanimate objects or forms.

Brise Soleil
A device that is used to reduce the sunlight entering a building and is applied to the building façade.

Collage
Collage derives from the French term *coller* (to stick). It was a technique that Cubist artists, such as Picasso, used in the 1920s. Collage can be applied to architectural concepts that use elements or references from other ideas, to create a new architectural piece.

Computer Aided Design (CAD)
Computer Aided Design is the use of computers and specially designed software to design and develop architecture and produce architectural representation.

Concept
This can be described as an initial idea that informs the development of the architectural design. The best concepts can be read clearly at the end of the architectural project in the detail, the plan and the overall interpretation of the building.

Context
In architectural terms, context refers to the setting or placing of the architecture.

Figure Ground
The idea of looking at maps of a city that reveal the figure or form of buildings as separate entities from the ground or space around them. It is a concept most famously used by Nolli in Rome in 1748. This allowed spaces to be read in cities separately from the buildings around them.

Free Plan
This concept originates from Le Corbusier and reflects his idea of using a frame structure for building: the Dom-ino frame. This liberates the internal spaces and allows elements such as walls to be located freely within the plan.

Genius Loci
This term refers to the spirit or essence of place. A piece of architecture can relate positively to the genius loci.

Hierarchy
In architectural application a hierarchy is an ordering of space, idea or form. Spaces can have more or less relative importance in a plan or building. Making spaces or elements physically larger or smaller suggests relative importance.

Layering
Layers can explain architecture at many levels. Physically spaces can be designed as layers so that one moves from the outside of a building through to the inside spaces and identifies each layer separately from another. Modernist spaces such as the Barcelona pavilion attempt to break down layers between inside and outside space.

Metaphor
Architectural metaphors are used at the concept stage of designing buildings. Le Corbusier has used the phrase 'a building as a machine for living'. Some metaphors are associated with form and others are more derivative.

Sophisticated metaphors as concepts are subtle rather than literal. A building inspired by a boat will not necessarily resemble a boat physically. It may, however, have boat-like references to material, shape and manufacture.

Module
Modules or measuring systems are essential in architecture. A module could be a brick or a human hand or a millimetre. It needs to be consistent and recognisable. Le Corbusier's Le Modulor uses geometry and anthropometrics to create a proportional measuring system.

Order
This refers to the range of classical columns; the five orders are Doric, Ionic, Corinthian ,Tuscan and Composite.

Parti
This represents a drawing which reduces an architectural idea to a diagram as a plan, section and/or elevation. The essence of this drawing is that the diagram is simple; it identifies the key issues of the architectural idea.

Piloti
This was used by Le Corbusier and is a French term to describe the columns that raise the building off the ground.

Place
For architecture, place is more than a site or location of a building. A place has physical definitions, it exists somewhere and can be described as geographical coordinates and map references. However, 'place' is about establishing the identity of a location or site, describing spiritual and emotional aspects of the site. Architects are involved in creating 'places', using the physical site as a platform.

Prefabrication
Fabrication describes the process of making objects in a controlled environment, such as a factory. Prefabrication involves the making of large-scale elements that can then be brought to a building site and assembled. These elements can range in scale from a kitchen or bathroom, to a house. Prefabrication allows quick installation and quality control, however it involves large amounts of planning and programming of installation.

Promenade
An architectural promenade derives from Le Corbusier and his idea of a controlled sequenced journey through a building that can act as an architectural device. It provides an order, axis and direction to the architectural idea.

Proportion
Describes the pleasing relationship between elements of an architectural idea or a building design and the whole. Proportioning systems were used in the classical and Renaissance period that related to the human body and the application of geometry.

Scale
Scale is about understanding the relative size of buildings and elements in recognised systems. Drawings and other information have to be prepared to recognised scales to allow buildings to be understood and built. These scales are expressed as a proportion of full size and are usually in metric or imperial.

Serial Vision
In *Townscapes*, Gordon Cullen refers to the idea of expressing movement through a city as a series of views or serial vision, to allow an idea of a journey to be described as views or sketch perspectives. It is a very useful device to describe a large building or urban space from an experiential point of view.

Servant / Served
Louis Kahn used this term to describe the contrasting types of space in architecture. The servant spaces are functional, housing services such as lifts, stairs, toilets, kitchens, ventilation units, heating systems and corridors. Served spaces are those that are experienced and celebrated, the living spaces of a house, the exhibition spaces of a gallery. There is a clear hierarchy between these spaces.

Storyboarding
This is a technique used in comic strip and film design to explain a narrative or story as a series of images or stills. It is a very useful planning device for architects to use to sequence an idea or concept of a building and allows them to plan a visual presentation or a journey though a series of designed spaces.

Tectonic
Tectonics describes the science of construction. Technology applies to all ideas of construction and manufacture.

Threshold
Originally the idea of crossing a threshold was to step into a space or territory, as a threshold represents a transition from one space to another. Usually the transition is from inside to outside, but it can be used to describe definitions between internal spaces. Thresholds are normally identifiable and marked; traditionally this was by a stone step, but a change or exaggeration of material at ground level identifies the threshold point.

Typology
This refers to classifications or models of understanding and description. In architecture buildings tend to belong to certain groups; these can be associated with form, function or both. Housing, schools, civic buildings, galleries, museums can all be described as typologies associated with function.

Wrapping
The way in which a wall can be clearly understood to 'wrap' around a simple space.

Zeitgeist
This literally translates as the 'spirit of the age'. It is in terms of architecture something that transcends the moment and refers to an idea that is broad and all encompassing culturally.

Zoomorphic
Ideas that are informed by animal shapes are referred to as zoomorphic. They may be inspired by physical forms or by material aspects.

Picture Credits

Introduction

Page 9, image 1
Courtesy of Foster + Partners and copyright of Richard Davies

Page 10, image 3
Courtesy and copyright of Jan Derwig / RIBA Library Photographs Collection

Page 11, image 4
Courtesy of David Cau

Chapter One

Page 13, image 1 dRMM
Courtesy of dRMM Architects

Page 15, image 2
Courtesy and copyright of Thomas Reichart

Page 15, image 3
Courtesy and copyright of Graham Tomlin

Page 16, image 4
Courtesy of Matt Swanton

Page 18, image 6
Courtesy of Alex Zambelli

Page 18, image 8
Courtesy of Robert Moore

Page 19, image 9
Courtesy of Paul Craven Bartle

Page 20, image 10
Courtesy of Rosie Danby

Page 23, image 14
Courtesy of Simon Astridge

Page 23, image 16
Courtesy and copyright of Design Engine Architects

Page 29, image 21
Courtesy of Simon Astridge

Page 29, image 22
Courtesy and copyright of Bernard Tschumi

Page 30, image 23
Courtesy and copyright of Bernard Tschumi

Page 33, image 27
Courtesy Richard Rogers Partnership
Copyright Katsuhisa Kida

Chapter Two

Page 35, image 1
Courtesy of Colin Graham

Page 43, image 5
Courtesy and copyright of George Saumarez Smith and Robert Adam Architects

Page 47, image 9
Courtesy of Emma Liddell

Page 49, image 10
Courtesy of Simon Astridge

Page 50, image 11
Courtesy of Khirman Vladimir

Page 52, image 12
Courtesy of Martin Pearce

Page 53, image 13
Courtesy of Valeriy Kalyuzhnyy

Page 54, image 14
Courtesy of Andy Linden

Page 58, image 18
Courtesy and copyright of RIBA Library Photographs Collection

Page 59, images 18 and 19
Courtesy of Eleanor Suess

Page 60, image 20
Copyright FLC/ADAGP, Paris and DACS, London 2006

Page 61, image 21
Courtesy and copyright of Jan Derwig / RIBA Library Photographs Collection

Chapter Three

Page 63, image 1
Courtesy and Copyright of Morphosis Architects

Page 63, image 2
Courtesy of Eleanor Suess

Page 65, image 3
Courtesy of Caruso St John Architects LLP. Copyright Héléne Binet

Page 66, image 4
Courtesy of Panter Hudspith Architects
Copyright Héléne Binet

Page 67, image 5
Courtesy and copyright of RIBA Library Photographs Collection

Page 69, image 8
Courtesy of Roger Tyrell

Page 69, image 9
Courtesy of Robert Moore

Page 70, image 10
Courtesy of Michael Stokes

Page 71, image 13
Courtesy and copyright of Pedro Varela

Page 73, image 13
Courtesy of Martin Pearce

Page 74, image 14
Courtesy of Simon Astridge

Page 74, image 15
Courtesy of Mike Liu

Page 75, image 17
Courtesy of David Yearley

Page 76, image 18
Courtesy and copyright of
David Mathias & Peter Williams

Page 79, image 22
Courtesy of Nick Hopper

Page 81, image 23
Courtesy of Jarno Gonzalez
Zarraonandia

Page 81, image 24
Courtesy of Presiyan Panayotov

Page 85, image 26
Courtesy of Matt Mardell

Chapter Four

Page 87, image 1
Courtesy of Robert Moore

Page 90, image 4
Courtesy of Robert Moore

Page 91, image 6
Courtesy of Gavin Berriman

Page 92, Image 7
Courtesy of the Serpentine Gallery
Copyright of Richard Bryant

Page 93, image 10
Courtesy of Colin Graham

Page 95, images 13 and 14
Courtesy of Gavin Berriman

Page 101, image 21
Courtesy and copyright of
John Pardey Architects

Page 102, image 22
Courtesy and copyright of
John Pardey Architects

Page 103, image 23
Courtesy and copyright of
John Pardey Architects

Page 105, image 25
Courtesy of Jeremy Davies

Page 107, image 29
Courtesy of Jeremy Davies

Page 109, image 32
Courtesy of Jayne Bannister

Page 111, image 34
Courtesy and copyright of
Zaha Hadid Architects

Page 112, image 34
Courtesy of Gavin Berriman

Page 112, image 35
Courtesy of Tom Heatherington/
Andy Young/Will Campbell

Page 112, image 36
Courtesy and copyright of
Design Engine Architects

Page 112, image 37
Courtesy of Ollie Wood

Page 115, images 38 and 39
Courtesy and copyright of
David Mathias & Peter Williams

Page 118/119, image 40
Courtesy of Nicola Crowson

Page 121, image 43
Courtesy of Nicola Crowson

Page 122, image 44
Courtesy of John Pardey Architects

Page 122, image 45
Courtesy of and copyright of
Design Engine Architects

Page 123, image 46
Courtesy of Panter Hudspith Architects

Page 123, image 47
Courtesy of Matt Swanton

Page 123, image 48
Courtesy of Make Architects

Chapter Five

Page 125, image 1
Courtesy and copyright of Lost Studio

Page 126, image 2
Courtesy of Martin Pearce
Page 127, images 3 and 4
Courtesy of Martin Pearce

Page 128, images 5 and 6
Courtesy of Martin Pearce

Page 129, images 7 and 8
Courtesy of Martin Pearce

Page 134, image 12
Courtesy of Cornel Archives

Page 135, image 14
Courtesy of Rocky Merchant

Page 136, image 15
Courtesy of Zaha Hadid Architects
Copyright Christian Richters

Page 137, image 16
Courtesy of Mark Himmens

Page 139, image 17
Courtesy of Simon Detjen Schmidt

Page 140, image 20
Courtesy of Roger Pilkington

Page 141, image 21
Courtesy of Darryl Sleath

Chapter Six

All images courtesy and copyright of
Design Engine Architects

Conclusion

Page 167, image 1
Courtesy and copyright of David Mathias

All reasonable attempts have been made to trace, clear and credit the copyright holders of the images reproduced in this book. However, if any credits have been inadvertently omitted, the publisher will endeavour to incorporate amendments in future editions. Unless otherwise cited all images are courtesy of the author and the University of Portsmouth School of Architecture.

Index

(Page numbers in *italics* denote illustrations. Entries in *italics* denote publication and films.)

Acknowledgements

This book required the knowledge and support of a variety of individuals, organisations and resources. Special thanks are due to Martin, Tom and Ellen for their encouragement throughout.

Thanks are also due to the staff and students of the University of Portsmouth's School of Architecture, who have supplied images, references and useful additional information; particular thanks are owed to Karl, Nicola and Michelle. Also special thanks to Simon Astridge for his picture research work.

Thanks also to Design Engine Architects, and in particular Richard Jobson, for offering to provide the information for the project featured in Chapter 6.

Thanks are also due to previous tutors who have provided inspiration, in particular Barry Russell and Jay Potts.

The idea of providing an introductory text to the subject has been an objective since I started to teach first year architecture, so, finally I'd like to say thank you to Caroline Walmsley and Brian Morris at AVA Publishing, who offered me the opportunity to write and have been consistently supportive and encouraging throughout the development of the book.

he Fundamentals of Architecture
orraine Farrelly

An AVA Book
Published by AVA Publishing SA
Rue des Fontenailles 16
Case Postale
1000 Lausanne 6
Switzerland
Tel: +41 786 005 109
Email: enquiries@avabooks.ch

Distributed by Thames & Hudson (ex-North America)
181a High Holborn
London WC1V 7QX
United Kingdom
Tel: +44 20 7845 5000
Fax: +44 20 7845 5055
Email: sales@thameshudson.co.uk
www.thamesandhudson.com

North American Support Office
AVA Publishing
Tel: +1 908 754 6169
Fax: +1 908 618 1172
Email: enquiries@avabooks.ch

English Language Support Office
AVA Publishing (UK) Ltd.
Tel: +44 1903 204 455
Email: enquiries@avabooks.ch

ISBN 2-940373-48-5 and 978-2-940373-48-2

10 9 8 7 6 5 4 3 2

Design by Gavin Ambrose

Production by AVA Book Production Pte. Ltd., Singapore

Tel: +65 6334 8173
Fax: +65 6259 9830
Email: production@avabooks.com.sg